Structural Innovation for Inclusive Development in Bihar

AUTHOR

Harsh Singh has a rich cross-institutional background. He served in the Indian Economic Service for a decade which included a tenure in the Department of Economic Affairs, Government of India. He served in UNDP India from 1992 to 2009. As Assistant Resident Representative, he led various Divisions such as Strategic Planning, Pro-poor Livelihoods and Private Sector Partnership. He also served as an advisor in the High Level Commission on Legal Empowerment of the Poor. He now heads the Centre on Market Solutions to Poverty at the International Management Institute, New Delhi.

Structural Innovation for Inclusive Development in Bihar

The Navodaya Shahar Model

HARSH SINGH

ACADEMIC FOUNDATION
NEW DELHI

www.academicfoundation.com

First published in 2012
by

ACADEMIC FOUNDATION
4772-73 / 23 Bharat Ram Road, (23 Ansari Road),
Darya Ganj, New Delhi - 110 002 (India).
Phones : 23245001 / 02 / 03 / 04.
Fax : +91-11-23245005.
E-mail : books@academicfoundation.com
www.academicfoundation.com

Cataloging in Publication Data--DK
Courtesy: D.K. Agencies (P) Ltd. <docinfo@dkagencies.com>

Singh, Harsh.
Structural innovation for inclusive development in Bihar : the Navodaya Shahar model / Harsh Singh.
p. cm.
Includes bibliographical references (p.).
ISBN 13: 9788171889242
ISBN 10: 8171889247

1. Rural development--Government policy--India--Bihar. 2. Land reform--India--Bihar. 3. Bihar (India)--Economic policy. I. Title.

DDC 307.14120954123 23

Typeset by Italics India, New Delhi.
Printed and bound in India.

I dedicate this book to my parents,
late Shri Ram Niwas Singh and late Smt Kaushalya Devi

Also, I owe special thanks to:

Shri S. Varadachary (Retd. IAS 1964, Kerala), my former supervisor in the Ministry of Finance, my mentor and guru

and

Rajshree, my better half

Contents

List of Tables, Figures and Boxes 11

Abbreviations 15

Preface 17

1. Introduction **19**

- *1.1 Need for a New Inclusive Growth Model for Bihar*
- *1.2 The Structural Context*
- *1.3 The Policy Challenge*
- *1.4 The Navodaya Shahar Model*
- *1.5 The Chapterisation Scheme*

2. State of the Triple Bottom Line of the *Aam Admi* in Rural Bihar **41**

- *2.1 Introduction*
- *2.2 The Breadth and Depth of Multidimensional Poverty in Bihar*
- *2.3 The Land Question*
- *2.4 The Education Sector*
- *2.5 The Health Sector*
- *2.6 Occupational Structure*
- *2.7 Need for a 'Land Reform Plus' Approach to Uplift the Triple Bottom Line of the Aam Admi*

3. Fragile Base of the New Resurgent Bihar **75**

- *3.1 Resurgence Post-2005*
- *3.2 Agriculture*
- *3.3 State of the Rural Enterprises*

3.4 *Banking Infrastructure, Deposits and Credit*

3.5 *Development Expenditure: Trends and Priorities for Pro-Poor Development*

3.6 *Conclusion*

4. Urbanisation Pattern and Implications for Rural Growth 99

4.1 *Trends in Urbanisation in Bihar*

4.2 *Lopsided Distribution of Urbanisation across Size-Class of Cities and Districts in Bihar*

4.3 *Urban Policy, Reforms and Programmes*

4.4 *Conclusion*

5. Outmigration and Implications for Inclusive Growth Strategies in Bihar 121

5.1 *Bihar and Migration*

5.2 *Trends in Outmigration from Bihar*

5.3 *Composition of Outmigrants and Factors Affecting Outmigration*

5.4 *Reasons for Outmigration*

5.5 *Remittances*

5.6 *Use of Remittances*

5.7 *Perception on Development Requirements at the Origin*

5.8 *Need for Long-Term Policy on Outmigration*

6. The Navodaya Shahar Model 137

6.1 *The Navodaya Shahar Model: An Overview*

6.2 *Homegarden Plots: The Evidence based on Multiple Benefits*

6.3 *The 'Ideal' Size of Homegarden Plots*

6.4 *Possible Impact of Large Programmes for Creation of Homegarden Plots on the Availability of Arable Land, Overall Agricultural Productivity and Food Security*

6.5 *Homegarden Plots: Implications in the Indian Context*

6.6 *Comparing the Recommendations of the Bihar LRC and the Navodaya Shahar Model*

6.7 *Can Navodaya Shahars be Created Given the Current Impasse on Land Acquisition?*

6.8 *The Management Challenge*

6.9 *Will Navodaya Shahars be able to Create a Livelihood Base, in say 3 to 5 Years?*

6.10 *The Navodaya Shahar Model versus the Strategy of Developing/Improving Services in the Existing District Towns, Block Headquarters and Other Small Towns*

6.11 *Likely Impact of Navodaya Shahars on Services across Rural Areas*

6.12 *The Navodaya Shahar Model versus the Traditional Urbanisation Approach*

6.13 *The Navodaya Shahar Model versus the Government of India's Flagship PURA Initiative*

7. Conclusions and Policy Implications 161

7.1 *Introduction*

7.2 *Evolving a 'Land Reform Plus' Agenda based on LRC Recommendations and the Roadmap for Agriculture: The Navodaya Shahar Model*

7.3 *Public-Private-Community Partnership (PPCP)*

7.4 *Leveraging National Programmes*

7.5 *Policy on Migration*

7.6 *Towards an Integrated Bihar Nav-Nirman Programme*

References 171

List of Tables, Figures and Boxes

Tables

2.1 Multidimensional Poverty across Indian States 45

2.2 Acute Multidimensional Poverty across States 46

2.3 Distribution (per 1,000) of Households by Type of House Structure 47

2.4 Distribution (per 1,000) of Households by Type of House Structure 49

2.5 Distribution of Rural Households by the Size Class of Land Possessed 51

2.6 Distribution of Rural Households (per 1,000) by Household Type 52

2.7 Percentage of Population, Mean Consumption and Land Ownership by Social Class 52

2.8 Availability of Schools in Relation to Population 61

2.9 Number of Patients Visiting Government Hospitals 65

2.10 Trend in Selected Health Indicators 66

2.11 Health Infrastructure Shortfall 69

2.12 Overview of Public Expenditure in Health Sector 69

2.13 WPR (per 1,000) according to Usual Status (PS+SS) by MPCE Quintile Classes 71

3.1 Yearly Growth Rate of GSDP (2005-06 to 2010-11 at 2004-05 Prices) 76

3.2 Achievement of DIC under Different Programmes 84

3.3 Progress in PMEGP 2010-11 85

3.4 CD Ratio of All Banks in Bihar 87

3.5 Bank Group-wise and Area-wise CD Ratio in Bihar 88

3.6 Distribution of Branches of Commercial Banks among States 90

3.7 Distribution of Commercial Bank Branch Offices in Bihar 90

3.8 Branches and Deposits of Regional Rural Banks 91

3.9 Cumulative Disbursements under RIDF till March 2010 92

3.10 Trend in Expenditure on Social and Economic Services 95

3.11 Extent of Disparity in Public Expenditure across Districts 96

4.1 Trends in the Level and Rate of Urbanisation across Major States 100

4.2 Proportion (Percentage) Urban Population to Total Population (2011-2026): Projection by the GoI Expert Committee 101

4.3 Bihar: Selected Demographic Indicators District-wise 103

4.4 Lifetime Net Migration Rate per 100 Population in Rural and Urban Areas by Sex (2001) (PoB Criteria) 105

4.5 Class-wise Distribution of the Towns/Cities (State-wise) Yet to be Covered by JNNURM and UIDSSMT for 15 Major States 114

4.6 Funds Released to Allocations under Urban Development Schemes (JNNURM + UIDSSMT) 116

4.7 State-wise Annual Per Capita Spending (Rs) by the Central Government on Different Components of Urban Development Schemes Meant for Mission and Non-Mission Cities/Towns since 6 December 2005 117

5.1 Proportion (per 1,000) of Households Reporting Outmigration 122

5.2 Profile of Respondents 124

5.3 Distribution (per 1,000) of Outmigrants by Reason for Outmigration 125

5.4 Remittance and Average Amount of Remittance Received per Household during 2007-08 126

5.5 Remittances by Different Social Groups 127

5.6 Proportion of Households (per 1,000) Using Remittance for Specific Purpose (State-wise) (Rural) 130

5.7 Proportion of Households (per 1,000) Using Remittance for Specific Purpose (State-wise) (Urban) 131

5.8 Use of Remittances 132

5.9 Responses of Households on the Impact of Migration 133

5.10 Changes Needed at the Origin 135

6.1 Districts and Class II-IV Towns in States 139

6.2 Alternative Scenarios for Meeting the Land Reform Objectives of Bihar LRC 149

Figures

2.1 Comparison of Poverty Estimates based on Tendulkar Committee Report (2004-05): Bihar and India 41

2.2 Composition of Multidimensional Poverty Index (MPI) Developed by Oxford Poverty and Human Development Initiative 42

2.3 Multidimensional Poverty Index (MPI) across Indian States 44

2.4 Overview of Distribution of Land in Bihar 57

2.5 District Level Coverage under JBSY 67

2.6 Construction of Hand Pumps under the Central Rural Water Supply Programme 67

2.7 Bihar: Employment by Sector 71

3.1 CD Ratio of Major Indian States as of March 2010 88

3.2 Per Capita Deposits and Credits of SCBs as on 31st March 2010 89

3.3 Trend in per Capita Development Expenditure 95

4.1 2011 Census: Density of Population 102

Boxes

2.1 Housing and Sanitation in Rural Samastipur 48

2.2 Mainstream: Implement Bandyopadhyay Commission's Recommendations for Land Reforms 56

2.3 The Beautiful Tree 63

3.1 Creating a Vibrant Public-Private-Panchayat Partnership for Inclusive Growth through Inclusive Governance: Need for a New PPPP-based Agri-Extension Framework 81

4.1 Progress in the Urban Reform Agenda in Bihar 112

5.1 Remittances for Staying Afloat above the Poverty Line 128

5.2 Aggregate Volume of Migration Incomes Higher than State Government Revenue 133

6.1 Impact of Homegarden Plots on Family Income: Evidence Advanced by FAO 141

6.2 Need for a New PPP-based Architecture for Skill Development of the Masses 155

List of Abbreviations

ACC	Artisan Credit Card
ADB	Asian Development Bank
ASI	Annual Survey of Industries
BRGF	Backward Region Grant Fund
BRLP	Bihar Rural Livelihood Project
CDS	Current Daily Status
CII	Confederation of Indian Industries
DFID	Department for International Development
DIC	District Industries Centre
DLHS	District-Level Household and Facility Survey
EBC	Extremely Backward Caste
FAO	(UN) Food and Agriculture Organization
GoB	Government of Bihar
GoI	Government of India
GSDP	Gross State Domestic Product
HDI	Human Development Index
IIPA	Indian Institute of Public Administration
IAY	Indira Awas Yojana
IAS	Indian Administrative Service
IHD	Institute of Human Development
IHSDP	Integrated Housing and Slum Development Programme
IMR	Infant Mortality Rate
JNNURM	Jawaharlal Nehru National Urban Renewal Mission
KCC	Kisan Credit Cards

LRC	Land Reforms Commission (Bihar)
MNREGS	Mahatma Gandhi National Rural Employment Guarantee Scheme
MSME	Micro-small and Medium Enterprises
NABARD	National Bank for Agriculture and Rural Development
NCAER	National Council of Applied Economic Research
NSDP	Net State Domestic Product
NSSO	National Sample Survey Organisation
ODI	Overseas Development Institute
OPHI	Oxford Poverty and Human Development Initiative
PCDE	Per Capita Developmental Expenditure
PHC	Primary Health Centre
PMEGP	Prime Minister's Employment Generation Programme
PPP	Public-Private Partnership
PRI	Panchayati Raj Institution
REGP	Rural Employment Generation Programme
RIDF	Rural Infrastructure Development Fund
RRB	Regional Rural Bank
SCARB	State Cooperative Agricultural and Rural Development Bank
SCB	Scheduled Commercial Bank
SGSY	Swarnajayanti Gram Swarozagar Yojana
SHG	Self-Help Group
TE	Triennium Ending
UIDSSMT	Urban Infrastructure Development Scheme for Small and Medium Towns
UNDP	United Nations Development Programme
UPSC	Union Public Service Commission

Preface

As a student from Bihar facing the UPSC interview panel for the Indian Economic Service examination in 1981, I anticipated 'the question'. And, for sure, it came. 'Why is Bihar so poor despite its bountiful natural resource endowment?' If I recollect correctly, I blamed it on the feudal legacy. The answer seems to have hit the right chord with the panel, which incidentally included the towering economist, Dr Sukhmoy Chakravarty. I secured 60 per cent in the viva voce segment!

It should not come as a surprise to anyone that a full three decades down the line, this question looks far more daunting. Many layers have piled up on the foundation of the feudal legacy.

But this appears to be a very opportune moment to revisit the question. The pall of gloom and doom has given way to a new feeling of pride and resurgence. How deep will this momentum reach? Will the migrant train from Bihar come to a halt? Will the next green revolution sprout from this Gangetic plain?

Yet, some options stand blocked at the outset. For example, the route of rural-urban transformation which is the usual path to economic and social transformation is not available. The projections made in 2006 by the Expert Group on Population Projection set up by the National Commission on Population indicate that even after 20 years (i.e., in 2026) Bihar's rural-urban ratio will remain trapped at a shockingly low level of 12 per cent. The pressure on land is growing by the day thereby diminishing the prospects of reversing the assetlessness of the masses.

It is clear that Bihar will have to chart out its own new model of inclusive development. A new approach to structural transformation is required to reverse the vortex of multidimensional poverty.

This book outlines the 'Navodaya Shahar' model based on a new 'land reform plus' agenda to uplift the 'triple bottom line' of the *aam admi* in rural Bihar. 'Navodaya Gram' is an equally apt description.

While this story unfolds in the context of Bihar, it is equally representative of large parts of India, including pockets in the so called leading states. Convergent approaches for ownership of assets by the poor households and feasible solutions for services will provide a solid base for identity, livelihood with dignity and democracy. Thus to me, the Navodaya Shahar or Navodaya Gram is the 21st century incarnation of Mahatma Gandhi's 'Gram Swaraj' vision.

—Harsh Singh
Director
Market Solutions to Inclusion

1 Introduction

1.1 Need for a New Inclusive Growth Model for Bihar

The stream of adolescent girls cycling to school is a poignant indicator of resurgence in this long stagnant Hindi heartland of India. Confirming it in economic terms, the Government of India's *Economic Survey, 2010-11* states, 'the best performer in terms of growth during 2002-03 to 2008-09 was Gujarat, followed by Bihar, Orissa, Haryana, and Uttarakhand... interestingly, the best performer in 2008-09 was Bihar with a growth rate of 16.59 per cent' (GoI, 2011a).

Thus, at last, 'Prometheus' is shaking off his chains. But will this giant go on to win the long race to development?

Some powerful warning signals are clearly discernible. Across a number of parameters, the growth rates are beginning to show signs of friction against deeper structural fissures. For example, while the progress in education at the primary and upper primary levels has been spectacular, at the secondary and senior secondary levels, the dropout rates continue to be as high as 80 to 90 per cent. The growth rates in the agriculture sector continue to swing wildly from year to year. The credit-deposit (CD) ratio which not only reflects the current health of the economy but determines its future growth prospects, shows sluggishness at a dismal level of around 32 per cent.

In the meanwhile, certain demographic patterns have crept to unsustainable levels. The 2011 Census results show that Bihar has already reached the population projections made for 2016. Eight districts in Bihar (Begusarai, Darbhanga, Muzaffarpur, Saran, Sheohar, Sitamarhi, Siwan and Vaishali) have now surpassed the population density of 1,471 persons per square kilometre that the Patna district had reached in 2001. But their urbanisation ratio remains trapped at around 5 to 10 per cent as compared to 41.6 per cent in the Patna district in 2001. In other words, the population density in such districts is three to four times higher than the all-India average while their urbanisation ratio is three to four times lower than the all-India average.

In such a scenario, masses neither have access to expanding urban assets, livelihood opportunities and services nor enjoy the expansive living conditions and resource base that one expects in the rural countryside. Thus the vast rank of the assetless continues to swell. Floods of outmigration have provided a safety valve. But unless internal mobility is generated through rapid structural transformation, the human development baseline will not budge, nor will the spectre of mass poverty begin to thaw.

Bihar will have to create its own new model of inclusive development. Among other things, this will entail introduction of innovations that generate benefits normally associated with inclusive urban transformation out of a predominantly rural baseline. But this is not a matter of providing urban amenities in the existing rural habitats as some models in vogue seem to suggest—forget the cost of creating such amenities, their upkeep itself will be infeasible.

This challenge calls for evolution of a new habitat structure, and social and economic organisation which could create an asset base for the masses and set the ball rolling for human development services and livelihood opportunities in a rising concentric circle. Progressively this will lift the 'triple bottom line' of the *aam admi* to a new level.

The book outlines the Navodaya Shahar model to advance this new approach. Navodaya Gram is an equally apt description.

The motive force behind the Navodaya Shahar model is a new 'land reform plus' agenda that is designed to break the incredible log jam in the traditional land reforms approach.

1.2 The Structural Context

In Bihar, a number of powerful currents intersect to create a vortex of multidimensional poverty. According to the Multidimensional Poverty Index (MPI) developed by the Oxford Poverty and Human Development Initiative (OPHI), 81 per cent of Bihar's population is multi-dimensionally poor. Also, poverty in Bihar and Jharkhand is most intense—poor people are deprived in 60 per cent of the MPI's weighted indicators (OPHI, 2010).

Some of the main elements of the structural fault lines are outlined below.

First is the magnitude of assetlessness of the masses. The World Bank report, *Bihar: Towards a Development Strategy* states, 'in fact, 75 per cent of the rural poor in Bihar were landless or near landless in 1999-2000. This expanded by eight per cent since 1993-94' (World Bank, 2005). In Bihar, the impact of the above high ratio gets further magnified because of the much higher proportion of the workforce dependant on agriculture and allied activities as well as the high absolute numbers involved.

A similar picture emerges with respect to homestead which is the only asset that the poor households own and which is perhaps their only identity device. Recent NSS data shows that 23.1 per cent of the rural households in Bihar live in 'unserviceable *kutcha* houses' as compared to 5.0 per cent at the all-India level. Similarly, barely a quarter of the households have access to electricity for domestic use as against two-thirds at the all-India level (NSSO, 2009).

There is a strong link between social identity, landlessness and poverty. While this applies across India, the nexus is much more strongly entrenched in the case of Bihar. Thus the bulk of the poor in Bihar can be defined as 'structural poor'.

Second is the depth of deprivation in human development services. An OPHI study provides estimates of the proportion of people who are deprived in education and health indicators based on NHFS-3 data. In Bihar, as much as 52 per cent of the population is shown as deprived in terms of child school attendance. For the indicator on mortality, it marks 35 per cent of the population as deprived (Alkire and Santos, 2010). While there has been an improvement in both these areas in the recent past, Bihar continues to figure at the lower end of the spectrum.

Third, the urbanisation ratio in Bihar in 2011 is a dismal 11.3 per cent as against the national average of 31.16 per cent and 48.45 per cent in Tamil Nadu, the most urbanised state in India.

In 2001, Bihar had only 139 urban centres as compared to 832 in Tamil Nadu, 378 in Maharashtra, 375 in West Bengal, 704 in Uttar Pradesh and 394 in Madhya Pradesh. The relative shortfall becomes much sharper when normailsed with respect to the population sizes of different states.

The distribution of urban centres in Bihar across size classes and regions further exacerbates its skewed nature.

In 2001, Bihar hosting 8 per cent of India's population had only 139 urban centres. In what appears to be a case of double whammy, these limited urban resources are distributed in a highly skewed manner—about 50 per cent of Bihar's urban population is concentrated in Class I towns, with a significant concentration in Patna. Thus, the vast expanse of Bihar remains starved of rural-urban linkages which are considered to be the highways to growth.

1.3 The Policy Challenge

Some observations regarding the treatment of the above structural issues in the development discourses on Bihar and in the concerned policy circles are in order.

Need for Convergent Policy Action based on the 'Triple Bottom Line' of the *Aam Admi*

The first two structural issues referred to in the previous sub-section are on the policy radar and a lot of effort is being channelled into these areas. But there is a need to converge them under a more comprehensive structural transformation framework so that they build on intersectoral linkages and harness cross-thematic energy. This will provide a new dynamism and reduce the cost of transition. Such consolidation is also likely to garner both local ownership and broad political support—factors that are critical for carrying out structural changes.

Soon upon assuming power in 2005, the Chief Minister, Nitish Kumar sought to revive the initiative in land reforms. He set up the Bihar Land Reforms Commission (LRC) under the leadership of D. Bandyopadhyay (IAS retd.), one of the key architects of land reforms in West Bengal.

LRC submitted its report in 2008. Citing NSS data, the report points to a reverse trend of land concentration in Bihar. It recommended allottment of between 1 acre to 0.66 acre of ceiling surplus land to the lowest quintile of agricultural labourers consisting of 16.68 lakh households. The Report also asked for assignment of at least 10 decimals of land each to shelterless households of 5.48 lakh non-farm rural workers. The other main recommendation pertained to strengthening of the position of sharecroppers or *bataidars* (Mainstream, 2009). But the vital issue of land consolidation remained untouched.

The Commission's recommendations ran into heavy political headwinds and are reportedly in 'cold storage'. The following remarks by some international experts although made earlier and in a broader context, sums up the main issues. Neilson *et al.* (2006) noted in a FAO working paper, 'land reform to broaden rural land access is still desperately needed in India. An estimated 17 million rural households are still completely landless and another 42 million households own less than 0.5 acre. The problems, however, will not be solved by relying solely on traditional land reform tools aiming to provide multiple acres for each land-poor household. Such goals are ideal, but often not feasible in the current political and fiscal environment. The central and state governments need to expand the number and type of tools in the land reform toolkit and prioritise improving land access for the most needy—those who have no land...Providing landless households with homestead plots fulfills the government's land reform and rural housing objectives' (Neilson *et al.*, 2006).

This book flags the need for a new 'land reforms plus' agenda. This paradigm calls for not only equipping large number of households with small landholdings as recommended above by FAO, but also for instituting new mechanisms that lead to consolidation of small holdings into viable habitats. This will create conditions for their highly productive use as well as growth of complimentary human development and livelihood linkages. In other words, the policy package needs to go beyond just distributing land to creating viable service and livelihood platforms.

The new 'land reforms plus' agenda will require additional mechanisms such as purchase of land to meet the needs of large numbers.

Such mechanisms should, to the extent possible, be market-based so that they grow rapidly on their own merit and not depend excusively on political will or administrative action that may be difficult to mobilise.

In this context, consider the theme of education. By allocating as much as 60 per cent of its total budget in the education sector to strengthening village-level primary and upper primary schools, the state government has succeeded in transforming the baseline at this level in many of the districts. At the level of secondary education however, there has been no improvement in infrastructure and the dropout rates remain uniformly and significantly high for all social groups—above 80 per cent for general category students, above 85 per cent for ST students and above 90 per cent for SC students. Sooner than later, such conditions are likely to affect the motivation levels in the lower classes and undo some of the gains made.

Now, while a breakthrough in primary education was made by making the small village-level schools functional, a much larger and more organised infrastructure will be required for boosting secondary and senior secondary education. Such schools will have to cover a number of villages. But as commuting may be difficult especially for girls, suitable infrastructure in terms of hostels etc., may be required. The problem of senior teachers shifting base to villages is well known. Thus, improving secondary and senior secondary education will necessitate a network of intermediate-level habitats. Further, given the budgetary constraints, it will not be possible to bridge the large gap at the secondary and senior secondary education level through government schools alone. The many private schools which are springing up will have to be harnessed in an organised way. Again intermediate-level habitats will help in attracting private entrepreneurs to set up good quality and accredited schools at the secondary and senior secondary level.

A similar picture emerges with respect to the agriculture sector which is emerging as the top priority of the NDA government during its second term starting 2010. Chapter 3 shows that developing the agriculture sector in Bihar is not a sectoral agenda. A reorganisation of the entire rural economy, demography and society is required.

Thus, policymakers need to take note of the role of intersectoral linkages while devising inclusive growth strategies. An organised effort will also contribute to reducing the considerable risks that the vulnerable sections face. This book outlines the configuration of the new intermediate-level habitat structure that is required to carry out the pro-poor development objectives of the government and boost the 'triple bottom line' of the *aam admi*.

Intensifying Rural-Urban Linkages

Deep policy concern with the first two issues outlined above (*viz.*, assetlessnes and dismal human development baseline) is quite evident. But surprisingly, there appears to be a 'blind spot' with respect to the critical issue of stunted urbanisation.

Given the preponderantly rural nature of the population in the state and the high rural poverty ratio, the development discourse on Bihar seems to focus almost exclusively on rural stagnation. The abysmally low rate of urbanisation in Bihar and its skewed character are seen mainly as a symptom of rural stagnation. Thus, while one hears of some hues and cries on the dismal state of urbanisation in Bihar, and of late, some remedial measures have been launched, this vital pillar of transformation has not received the attention that it deserves in the state's inclusive growth agenda.

In its report, *India: Preparing the Bihar Urban Development Project*, the Asian Development Bank (ADB) comments on this policy shadow. It states, 'the state has yet to prepare a statement of its urban policy or strategy. Without such a unified policy document, urban sector works have been fragmentary and have been undertaken by different agencies without close alignment of resources, resulting in grossly inadequate and inefficient urban development...' (ADB, 2008).

There is a need to bring distributed urbanisation on the policy agenda as inclusive development on the desired scale will not be possible without it. Policymakers need to note the evidence emerging from some important recent studies. Based on an in-depth study of long-term trends, Ravallion and Datt of the World Bank conclude, 'we find much stronger evidence of a positive feedback effect from urban economic growth to rural poverty reduction than we had found in the pre-1991 data' (Datt and Ravallion, 2010). Similarly, another recent study concludes that galvanising small towns may serve both urban and rural poverty reduction objectives (Himanshu *et al.*, 2010).

The most conclusive evidence comes from Krishna and Bajpai (2011). Triangulating results from large household surveys conducted by the National Council of Applied Economic Research (NCAER) in 1993-1994 and in 2004-05, and the Census 1991 and 2001 figures, Krishna and Bajpai (2011) conclude, 'the distribution of benefits from economic growth since the early 1990s has followed an identifiable spatial pattern. People in the largest cities have achieved the greatest gains, followed by people in small towns and villages close to towns. Further away, in villages located more than five kilometres from the nearest town—home to more than half of the entire population of India—inflation-adjusted per capita incomes fell between 1993 and 2005. The steepest declines were experienced by the lowest income groups. Rising inequality is a natural result of these spatially distributed trends. The debilitating effects of 'distance from town' need to be countered by connecting outlying villages with more and better physical and social infrastructures.'

However, creating the desired rural-urban linkages in the vast rural expanse of Bihar is going to be a highly challenging task. First, the baseline is dismal. Thus, while the existing small towns and other urban centres in the interior hinterland need to be rejuvenated and expanded, given the humungous backlog, they will not be able to meet the needs of the vast rural masses. Second, given the high cost of land even in small towns and urban centres, it is unlikely that the rural poor will be able to find berth. Thus, Bihar will have to chart out its own model of distributed urban growth.

As indicated earlier, the projection for 2026 made by the Expert Group on Population Projection indicates that Bihar's rural-urban ratio will remain trapped at around 12 per cent as against the all-india average of 38.2 per cent while its population will rise to 11.38 crore from 8.29 crore in 2001. Consequently the urban size in Bihar will grow, but such growth will just manage to keep pace with the growing population. As a result the rural–urban structure of the 11.38 crore population in Bihar in 2026 will not have changed much.

The Navodaya Shahar model outlined in this book responds to this challenge. This model aims at creating new low cost 'rur-ban' habitats that help ameliorate the deprivation in terms of assets and also generate their own livelihood base by bridging the gap in the 'triple bottom line' of the *aam admi*. Such habitats are likely to set into motion a process of mobility for a large number of households into new livelihood streams. This in turn will generate a process of reorganisation of the land mass for agriculture towards its high potential yield. In other words, the Navodaya Shahar model would help overcome the dismal projections of the Expert Group by opening up a new route to rural-urban transformation.

1.4 The Navodaya Shahar Model

A survey was carried out by the National Council of Applied Economic Research (NCAER) in 2008 to capture the perceptions of poor households on their livelihood needs and development priorities. It covered 3,200 rural households in 16 backward districts in the seven lagging northern states (NCAER, 2008).

Three-fourths of those surveyed reported that sufficient work was not available for all the members of the household. Accessibility and satisfaction levels with regard to human development services showed a similar response. Remoteness of the location and poor connectivity emerged as major factors affecting the access to various social and economic programmes of the government.

Households reported that the three top factors for improving their capability were: more employment (83.1%), improved assets (64.1%) and better education (33.9%). This menu could be called the 'triple bottom line of the *aam admi*'.

Some recent studies on the size distribution of villages in India and its impact on the availability of services provide supplementary clues on the above 'triple bottom line'. The 2001 Census shows that out of a total of 5.94 lakh inhabited villages in the country, 1.28 lakh had population size of 200-499 persons. Another 1.45 lakh villages had 500-999 persons. In the study, 'Villages in India: How Relevant is it in the Context of Development?' the authors (Singh *et al.*, 2008) conclude that the index of development is positively related with the per cent of population living in large villages. Punjab and West Bengal emerge as the two exceptions. The authors caution, 'the number of small villages is very large, and the rate of movement of population observed in the study can only be of small help in transferring them into large ones.'

Thus models that spur viable habitats are required. Such habitats should not only provide an opportunity to equip the *'aam admi'* with assets having livelihood and growth potential, but also facilitate organisation of high quality human development services such as education and health at reasonable cost and easy reach. Ownership of productive assets will create a certain secure livelihood base. The large unmet needs for human development services and other opportunities in and around the growing habitat will progressively transform themselves into a major source of livelihood. Thus many of the elements of the so called urban pull will be realised while sustaining close connectivity with rural life and livelihood opportunities.

At the core of this model is distribution of home and garden plots of 380 square metres to each landless household. This modality is based on the comprehensive evidence base built up by FAO and the Rural Development Institute, Washington DC on the multiple benefits from such home and garden plots. For example, homegardens in Russia comprised about 4.5 per cent of total agricultural land in 2000, and yet were reported to have produced 64 per cent of all produce in the country, including 90 per cent of all potatoes and 75 per cent of fresh vegetables (Borisova, 2000 cited in FAO). In China, until the collectives were broken up, small plots were allowed on some 5 per cent of arable land, and produced 15–20 per cent of the total value of agricultural production (Prosterman, 2010). In Karnataka, on well-developed homegarden plots of about 0.07 acre (about 300 m^2 or 3,000 ft^2), apart from direct household consumption, these households received an average Rs 11,000 of annualised income from the sale of products from their plot. This was equivalent to earnings from 200-220 days of agricultural labour, or somewhat more than a typical annual wage for an adult male working fulltime in the field (Hanstad *et al.*, 2008 cited in Prosterman, 2010). In a study of Kerala wage earning families who cultivate homegarden plots occupying a fraction of an acre, Kumar (1978) found that the value of homegarden production was the most consistent positive predictor of child nutrition. A survey of rural households in

Karnataka revealed that among households that had received small plots to construct homes and gardens, increased status within the village was the most cited benefit of ownership, surpassing even income and nutritional benefits. Poorer households cited increased status even more often than other households (Hanstad *et al.*, 2002 cited in FAO).

The state governments are implementing programmes for securing land for the landless. Besides accessing the land pool in their possession, they have bought land from the market for this purpose. However, often such land parcels are scattered across remote locations, and in the absence of supplementary inputs, the beneficiaries are not able to utilise such assets. Similarly, there are a number of programmes such as the Indira Awas Yojana (IAY) which support the poor households in constructing houses.

The convergent 'triple bottom line' paradigm outlined in this book calls for re-organising such land distribution, housing construction and human development initiatives to spur viable habitats. Borrowing a leaf from the Navodaya School initiative, these habitats could be called Navodaya Shahars. Navodaya Grams could be an equally apt description.

Navodaya Shahars are visualised as habitats of around 5,000 households each so that a critical minimum size is reached for the provision of quality human development services such as middle and higher secondary schools at par with the Navodaya Schools, skill development centres, quality health services etc. Assuming that 5 per cent of the land will be used to construct roads, drainage, public schools and hospitals etc., a one hectare plot could provide 380 metre square plots to 25 families. Taking a land cost of Rs 2-3 lakh per acre in the deep rural hinterland, the cost of each plot is likely to be Rs 20,000 to 30,000. This is comparable to the subsidy element in a number of poverty alleviation and social security programmes such as the Indira Awas Yojana.

Navodaya Shahars need to be located deep in the countryside where the penetration of human development services is highly deficient. The typical symptoms of this scenario include high dropout rates at the middle school level and low rate of institutional delivery leading to high rates of maternal and infant mortality.

Such habitats could be developed through planned upgradation of small existing rural *kasbas* which have connectivity and growth potential. To enable households to progressively set foot into new opportunities while maintaining links with their traditional livelihoods and social network, each Navodaya Shahar should have a catchment radius of not more than 10-12 km. This would translate into a requirement of around 9 or 10 Navodaya Shahars in a district.

While starting with the blueprint of a well-planned habitat, a modular approach to rollout of amenities needs to be adopted. In terms of social infrastructure, the first charge should be on creating human development services such as education, skill development and health services. In terms of physical infrastructure, while the main arterial connectivity could be created upfront, amenities such as internal lanes etc., could be built up progressively in tandem with the growing economic baseline of the habitat. The idea is to conserve resources and keep costs to the minimum so that large number of low income households are covered.

The Bhujuria artisan hamlet located 15-20 km from Bhuj in Gujarat is an example of organic growth along these lines. Initially, the artisans settled here in plot sizes of a quarter acre or so. They built *katcha* houses, allocated some space for their cattle and put in a shed or two for their looms. With economic prosperity, houses have become *pucca*, and often new units for married children have been added. Also, shops to display and sell local handicraft have come up in many of the houses. Similarly, the roads etc., are being steadily upgraded. The result is a bustling habitat that combines the best of rural and urban features.

Public agencies will have to take a lead in human development services such as education, skill development and health care. But if an enabling policy framework for public-private participation (PPP) is created, a fountain of people's own enterprise will erupt to take the services etc., to a new growth path. The models proposed in Chapter 6 provide for 25 to 50 per cent additional land for this purpose.

A similar PPP approach could be invoked for the mobilisation of land for creation of Navodaya Shahars. Existing landholders could be incentivised to pool in their land for plotting at reasonable rates through promise of attractive returns on many new opportunities that are likely to emerge.

Various studies and surveys bear out that even in the context of backward districts, around three-fourths of the households own their house (though mostly *katcha*). Similarly, a good proportion of these households own very small pieces of land. Thus, if secure mechanisms for formalising such assets are created, many of the households will be able to set foot into the new habitats based on their own assets, own choice and at their own pace. Covering such habitats under the Indira Awas Yojana, MNREGS and other relevant public programmes will further support the poorest in securing a plot and developing it. Cash transfers in an organised manner could play a truly transformational role in this setting by providing the cushion to the poor households to tide into the new setting. But overall, in this model, the 'bang' comes not from the resources as such, but from its organising principle.

Will creation of Navodaya Shahars on a large scale reduce the availability of arable land and exacerbate food security concerns? FAO's estimates allay such fears. As indicated earlier, according to FAO, the nation's estimated 15 million completely landless families could be provided 380 metre square plots each by redeploying only 4/10th of 1 per cent of the nation's arable land (FAO).

Chapter 6 on the Navodaya Shahar model compares it with the Government of India's flagship programme on 'Provision of Urban Amenities in Rural Areas' or PURA and concludes that the former approach is much more relevant for the development baseline of Bihar.

Citizens have a right to demand equitable development opportunities in their existing habitats. But equally important is the opportunity for choices, including the choice of mobility that is conducive to new opportunities and improved human development services. The Navodaya Shahar model presented in this book needs to be seen in this light.

Many of the backward districts across the lagging states have urban ratios below 10 per cent. A planned effort to double their urban/ru-rban population over the five years of the Twelfth Plan in line with the 'triple bottom line' approach inherent in the 'land reforms plus' approach will set in motion a chain reaction of inclusive growth. Chapter 6 shows the dramatic implications of the Navodaya Shahar model in transforming the 'rur-ban' share. Adopting it for the provision of land to 22.16 lakh landless families that the Bihar LRC drew attention to, will help create a network of around 350 habitats (Navodaya Shahars) or 9 per district. The total population size of these organised rur-ban habitats will be equal to the total existing urban population in Bihar. This will completely transform the rural baseline of Bihar.

Ownership of assets by the poor households and feasible solutions for services will provide a solid base for livelihood and democracy. Political commitment could transform the Navodaya Shahars or Navodaya Grams into the 21st century incarnation of Mahatma Gandhi's Gram Swaraj vision.

1.5 The Chapterisation Scheme

Chapter 2 explores the health of the 'triple bottom line' of the *aam admi* in rural Bihar *viz.*, landholding, quality of housing and amenities, the human development needs of education and health, and the occupational structure.

This chapter draws on the Multidimensional Poverty Index (MPI) developed by the Oxford Poverty and Human Development Initiative (OPHI). Interstate comparison of MPI indicators shows that the extent of deprivation in Bihar is much larger than what the traditional income or calorie consumption-based indicators seem to indicate. Four-fifths of Bihar's population falls in the category of multidimensionally poor and is deprived in atleast three of the 10 MPI indicators. Infact, the intensity of poverty in Bihar is very high as these households are deprived in 60 per cent of the MPI's weighted indicators.

This chapter outlines the state of landlessness in Bihar. It discusses the experience with land reforms. It analyses the recommendations of the recent Land Reforms Commission in Bihar and suggests the need for a new 'land reforms plus' agenda to not only equip large number of households with small holdings but also create conditions for their highly productive use through the growth of complimentary services and livelihood linkages.

Chapter 2 shows that as per the recent NSS data, 23.1 per cent of the rural households in Bihar are living in 'unserviceable *katcha* houses' (NSSO, 2009). These are the poorest of the poor, and in all likelihood, victims of multiple vulnerabilities—economic and social—in their own villages. This is also the segment that has not been able to participate equitably in the out of state migration activities due to their economic condition and poor social linkages. Navodaya Shahar-type interventions are required to open up options for safe and secure local mobility for this vulnerable section.

This chapter describes the spectacular achievements as well as shortfalls in the areas of education and health. Again, the need for a broader development approach to carry the gains to the next level emerges.

Chapter 3 discusses the recent trends in macroeconomic performance of the state as well as some of the sectoral trends in areas relevant to the Navodaya Shahar model. These areas are agriculture, the rural enterprise sector, the financial sector and public outlays for development.

It emerges that the recent buoyant trends remain fragile. The high sectoral growth rates show signs of resistance against structural fault lines. This leads to the conclusion that unless the structural fault lines are dissolved and the economic base widened by including large segments which currently languish in poverty, sustained growth will not be possible.

Agriculture seems have emerged as the top priority of the NDA government during its second term starting November 2010. In April 2011, the Chief Minister, Nitish Kumar set up the first of a kind 'special cabinet on agriculture' to draw up a model for the state. The 'special cabinet' has set up 14 committees that include subjects such as water, cooperative, agriculture, animal husbandry, fisheries, disaster management etc.

The analysis presented in this book, however, leads to the conclusion that given the population size dependant on agriculture, developing this sector in Bihar to its full potential is neither a purely technical matter nor a sectoral agenda. The reform canvass will have to be far broader than the kind of strategy deployed during the first green revolution *viz.*, concentration of inputs and facilities such as irrigation, credit and lucrative procurement prices. An all encompassing re-organisation of the rural economy and society will have to be initiated and nurtured. The Navodaya Shahar Model emerges as an important instrument in this regard.

Chapter 3 also shows that the rural industrialisation base remains highly weak. The overwhelmingly rural nature of most of the districts in the state and consequent lack of rural-urban linkages have tended to starve the enterprise sector from all sides—demand, inputs, credit, skilled labour, transport etc.

Lack of non-farm employment opportunities has meant that upon fragmentation of land or other agriculture-related shocks, a large part of the marginal farmers have had no option but to move into the ranks of landless labour. Women have tended to move out of the workforce. This in turn has further impoverished the base of rural enterprises. This chapter concludes that the growth of rural enterprises and that of distributed industrialisation more generally is again not a sectoral agenda.

This chapter enquires into the financial sector in Bihar in some depth as it determines the future growth prospects. Among the national-level financial institutions, disbursement of loans by NABARD under RIDF did not reach even half the total sanctioned amount. Progress made under anti-poverty schemes such as PMEGP and SGSY has been similarly annulled by extremely low rates of recovery.

The CD ratio in Bihar seems to be stagnating at a highly dismal level of 32 per cent. The *Bihar Economic Survey 2010-11* concludes, 'overall, it appears that banking in Bihar is yet to start creating a real impact on the investment climate in the state.'

Reaching the national average, CD ratio will generate additional investible resources of over Rs 30,000 crore. Success in attaining the CD ratio of Andhra Pradesh would translate into additional investible resources of Rs 65,000 to 70,000 crore which is equivalent of the total outlay for Bihar in the Eleventh Plan.

Again, lack of rural-urban linkages emerges as a key cause for deficient banking infrastructure in the rural sector. The recent trend shows a further decline in the rural share. The *Bihar Economic Survey 2010-11* indicates that during 2009-10, of the 214 new branches opened in Bihar, all but 44 were opened in either urban or semi-urban areas. Most of these new branches belonged to private banks.

The trend in public development expenditure shows that the state government is according high priority to social sectors. But the development budget of the state government is very small. On top of that, utilisation rates in many of the areas are highly suboptimal. There are large inter-district disparities. Thus, again there is a need to address the structural issues, particularly the rural-urban linkages so that public expenditure generates a multiplier effect.

Chapter 4 explores the urbanisation pattern in Bihar. But the agenda is not urban development *per se*. The objective of this analysis is to understand better the interplay between stunted urbanisation and rural stagnation, and to identify implications for human development and inclusive growth.

Bihar's urban sector is highly underdeveloped in relation to other states in India. As reported earlier, according to the 2011 Census, the urban ratio in Bihar at 11.3 per cent is only a third of the national average. In the decade 1971-1981, the rate of growth of urbanisation in Bihar was 4.3 per cent *vis-a-vis* the national average of 3.1 per cent. However, by 2001-2011, this rate has declined sharply to 0.76 per cent and stands below the national average of 1.21 per cent.

In 2001, Bihar hosting 8 per cent of India's population had only 139 urban centres. In what appears to be a case of double whammy, these limited resources are distributed in a highly skewed manner. About 60 per cent of Bihar's urban population is concentrated in the southern part of the state, with a significant concentration in Patna.

Thus the vast countryside of Bihar remains starved of rural-urban linkages that are considered to be the highways to growth and human development. The small size of the urban sector in the state also puts tremendous pressure on the infrastructure in the existing cities and towns. The result is low tolerance for settling-in population from the countryside. This shows up in abnormally high urban poverty rates in Bihar and high migration levels even from the urban areas of the state.

This Chapter also throws light on some key evidence regarding urban-rural linkages and on urban reforms underway in the state. While these reforms are much needed, the overall reform agenda remains quite narrow and focusses mainly on the larger urban centres. Also, the utilisation levels in many of the programmes remain highly sub-optimal.

As indicated earlier, the projection for 2006 made by the Expert Group on Population Projection indicates that Bihar's rural-urban ratio will remain trapped at around 12 per cent as against the all-india average of 38.2 per cent, while its population will rise to 11.38 crore from 8.29 crore in 2001. Consequently in 2026, the population density in Bihar will be almost three times higher than the all-India average. The 2011 Census delivers a further shock. It shows that Bihar has already reached the population projections made for 2016.

Thus, Bihar will have to create its own new model of inclusive development. Among other things, this will entail introduction of innovations that generate in a predominantly rural baseline, benefits normally associated with inclusive urban transformation. The Navodaya Shahar model seeks to advance this agenda.

Chapter 5 presents the story of peoples' struggle for survival through outmigration. Underneath this story lurks the pain of unsettled identity and insecure existence in distant places.

The analysis draws on the data from the NSS 64th Round (NSSO, 2010c) as well as some excellent recent studies by academicians from the Indian Institute of Public Administration or IIPA (Kumar and Banerji, 2010) and the Institute of Human Development or IHD (Bhaskaran and Mehta, 2010). The IIPA study was sponsored by the Government of Bihar.

According to the NSS 64th Round, 25.8 per cent of the rural households in Bihar reported outmigration in 2007-08. Other studies report much higher outmigration rates from Bihar. The IIPA study estimates that migration of labour from Bihar may be affecting about one-third of the rural households. The IHD study which traces migration from the Samastipur district of Bihar to Delhi concludes, 'in the sample population, one out of every three people had migrated to Delhi, indicating a high incidence of migration. Two out of three people who belonged to economically active age group (14-44 years) migrated, indicating a major imbalance in the supply or availability of able bodied.'

These studies conclude that people from backward and disadvantaged groups are more likely to migrate. The social composition of migrants finds its reflection in the occupational pattern of the migrating population.

The proportion of households receiving remittances is very high. The IIPA study notes, 'almost all (99%) the migrant households stated that they received remittances from the migrant member working outside...at their destination, the proportion of respondents replying in the affirmative to the question of sending remittances to their families was 90 per cent.'

As per the NSS, for rural Bihar, the average amount of remittances per household reporting receipt of remittances was Rs 15,148 during 2007-08. The findings by other studies match with this figure. As per NSS, nearly 75 per cent of the households used remittances for buying food. Thirty-seven per cent of the households used remittances for health support. The IIPA and IHD studies throw up some other priorities for the use of remittances such as debt clearance. Overall, only a small fraction of remittances is used for capital formation.

The IHD study reports that about 67.2 per cent of origin households wanted the migrants to return to the village and a similar ratio of the migrants ultimately plan to settle down in their origin village. However, lack of infrastructure in the origin villages and its impact on their socioeconomic conditions remains a deterrent. This chapter outlines the changes that migrants want in their villages. The Navodaya Shahar model seeks to create habitats that the migrants desire to return to once their earning objective has been fulfilled. On the other side of the coin, the migrant population with their very large resource base (income, skill base and enterprise) will be a key stakeholder in giving shape and vibrancy to Navodaya Shahars.

Chapter 6 presents the Navodaya Shahar model. The basic features of the model have already been covered under sub-section 1.4 above.

This chapter captures the comprehensive evidence base on reported benefits from the home and garden plot modality which is at the core of the Navodaya Shahar model.

The Central Government and a number of state governments including the Government of Bihar have launched programmes in this area.

But by and large, their scale and impact have been minimal. Most of these programmes underestimate the livelihood potential of the homegarden plots and over-estimate the costs—financial and the opportunity cost in terms of land use. Thus they miss out on the powerful development structure that can be built on this modality. This chapter presents arguments and evidence to show that these concerns are unfounded. As indicated earlier, according to FAO, in India, the nation's estimated 15 million completely landless families could be provided 380 square metre plots each by redeploying only 4/10th of 1 per cent of the nation's arable land (FAO).

Chapter 6 shows the dramatic implications of this new approach. Adopting it to for the provision of land to 22.16 lakh landless families that the Bihar LRC drew attention to, will help create a network of around 350 habitats (Navodaya Shahars) or 9 per district. Each habitat will have an average size of 5,000 households and occupy a compact area of about three square kilometres. These habitats will together consume less than one per cent of Bihar's total area, but create a network of organised 'rur-ban' habitats whose total population size will be equal to the total existing urban population in Bihar. While these models would bring down the land requirement *vis-à-vis* the estimates of Bihar LRC, their implications in terms of human development services and creation of livelihood opportunities will be incomparable. Implementation of such models with political committeemen could completely transform the rural baseline of Bihar.

This chapter outlines a PPP-based strategy for creation of Navodaya Shahars. It also responds to the typical questions and queries that were encountered while discussing the Navodaya Shahar model with scholars and practioners. Some of these are: Can Navodaya Shahars be created given the current impasse on land acquisition? Why not develop/improve services in the existing district towns and block headquarters instead of creating new habitats? Given budgetary constraints, will services in Navodaya Shahars be at the cost of their wider distribution across rural areas? How is the Navodaya Shahar model different from the traditional urbanisation approach? How does the Navodaya Shahar model relate to the Government of India's flagship initiative, Provision of Urban Amenities in Rural Areas (PURA)?

Chapter 7 outlines the policy implications of the 'land reform plus' agenda and the Navodaya Shahar model. It analyses the relevance of some of the major contemporary policy initiatives and programmes at the Central and state levels and explores the possible direction for their realignment. These include the land reforms agenda and the state's roadmap for agriculture, SGSY and its new incarnation, the National Rural Livelihood Mission (NRLM) as well as the much talked about modality of cash subsidies.

This chapter highlights the role of public-private community partnership in the context of the Navodaya Shahar model and stresses the need for strengthening of community capacity and property rights for the poor.

It also highlights the need for a long-term policy on migration as this modality is not likely to subside in the near future. Such policies need to support the migrants both at the point of destination and at the point of origin. While the former have been discussed in a number of recent studies, this book provides a new direction for the latter.

The change from a service delivery-driven approach to the 'triple bottom line' approach will require a major transformation in the existing administrative structure and development management system which have mounted incredible human misery. Particularly, the major rural-urban fault line within the government itself needs to be bridged as rigid bifurcation of government functioning into 'rural development' and 'urban development' strands seems to be creating a roadblock in what is meant to be a natural and seamless process in the lives of the *aam admi,* the business of societies, and in the political and economic decentralisation process.

This chapter calls for a new organising principle—the Bihar Nav-Nirman Programme to galvanise all resources for a joint attack on the spectre of mass multidimensional poverty.

2 State of the Triple Bottom Line of the *Aam Admi* in Rural Bihar

2.1 Introduction

Estimates on the incidence of poverty based on the Tendulkar Committee report suggest that rural Bihar is significantly behind the national average. Rural poverty in Bihar was estimated at 55.7 per cent in 2004-05 compared to the all-India average of 41.8 per cent.

Figure 2.1

Comparison of Poverty Estimates based on Tendulkar Committee Report (2004-05): Bihar and India

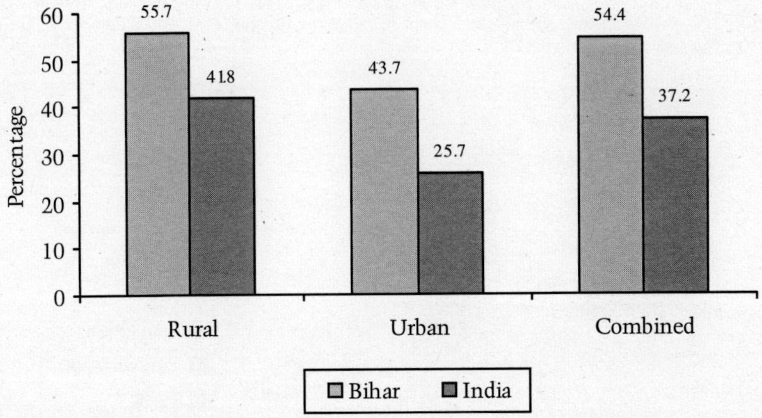

Source: *Bihar Economic Survey 2010-11*, Government of Bihar.

As per this new methodology, there are 90 lakh poor households in Bihar. This is significantly higher than 65 lakh poor households estimated earlier by the Planning Commission. Also, the rate of decline in poverty in Bihar appears to be slower than what was estimated earlier. Scholars broadly agree that the new poverty line is able to capture better the vulnerabilities. It includes 79 per cent of the illiterate households, 80 per cent of the agricultural labourer households and 75 per cent of the SC community in Bihar (IHD, 2010).

But even these higher estimates pale in front of the picture that emerges from a new methodology evolved to capture the multidimensional nature of poverty and its severity. Developed by the Oxford Poverty and Human Development Initiative (OPHI), the Multidimensional Poverty Index (MPI) uses 10 indicators to measure poverty in three dimensions: education, health and living standard. A person is identified as poor if she or he is deprived in at least 30 per cent of the weighted indicators (Alkire and Santos, 2010).

Figure 2.2

Composition of Multidimensional Poverty Index (MPI) Developed by Oxford Poverty and Human Development Initiative (OPHI)

Composition of the MPI

The MPI can be broken down to see directly how much each indicator contributes to multidimensional poverty. The following figure shows the composition of MPI using a pie-chart. Each piece of the pie represents the percentage contribution of each indicator to the overall MPI of the country. The larger the contribution the bigger is the weighted share of the indicator to the overall poverty.

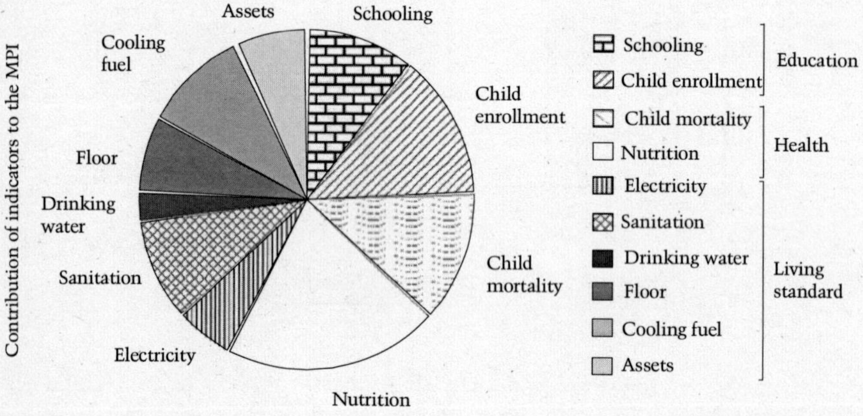

Source: OPHI (2010).

Studies under OPHI categorise 81 per cent of Bihar's population as multidimensionally poor and also show that poverty in Bihar and Jharkhand is most intense—poor people are deprived in 60 per cent weighted indicators in the MPI. Bihar's MPI is similar to Guinea's (the 8th poorest country in the global ranking). (OPHI, 2010).

This breadth and depth of deprivation in Bihar and its composition moves the development discussion from concerns with the coverage and quality of service delivery into structural issues.

Could vitality be imparted to the above indicators within the structural confines of the rural sector that is shorn of urban linkages? Could the individual elements of livelihood security be addressed separately, or is an integrated approach to tap their mutual synergy a necessary condition for triggering inclusive growth? How can such integration be achieved and what will be the appropriate platform for such integration? Particularly, how can the current service delivery-driven approach be combined with strengthening of the asset base of the *aam admi*? But given that the availability of land, which is the key asset in an agrarian society, is highly limited, how can the asset needs of large masses be met? These are the main points of enquiry in this chapter.

Section 2.2 outlines the breadth and depth of multidimensional poverty in Bihar. Section 2.3 discusses the land question. Sections 2.4 and 2.5 define the baseline in terms of human development services of education and health. Section 2.6 outlines occupational structure and transition. Section 2.7 discusses the need for a new 'land reforms plus' agenda to uplift the 'triple bottom line' of the *aam admi*.

2.2 The Breadth and Depth of Multidimensional Poverty in Bihar

The following interstate comparison of MPI indicators based on NFHS-3 data shows that the extent of deprivation in Bihar *vis-à-vis* other states in India is much larger than what the traditional calorie consumption-based measures and HDI indicate. The distance of its MPI score from other similarly placed states such as Andhra Pradesh, Rajasthan and Uttar Pradesh is quite large (OPHI, 2010).

Figure 2.3

Multidimensional Poverty Index (MPI) across Indian States

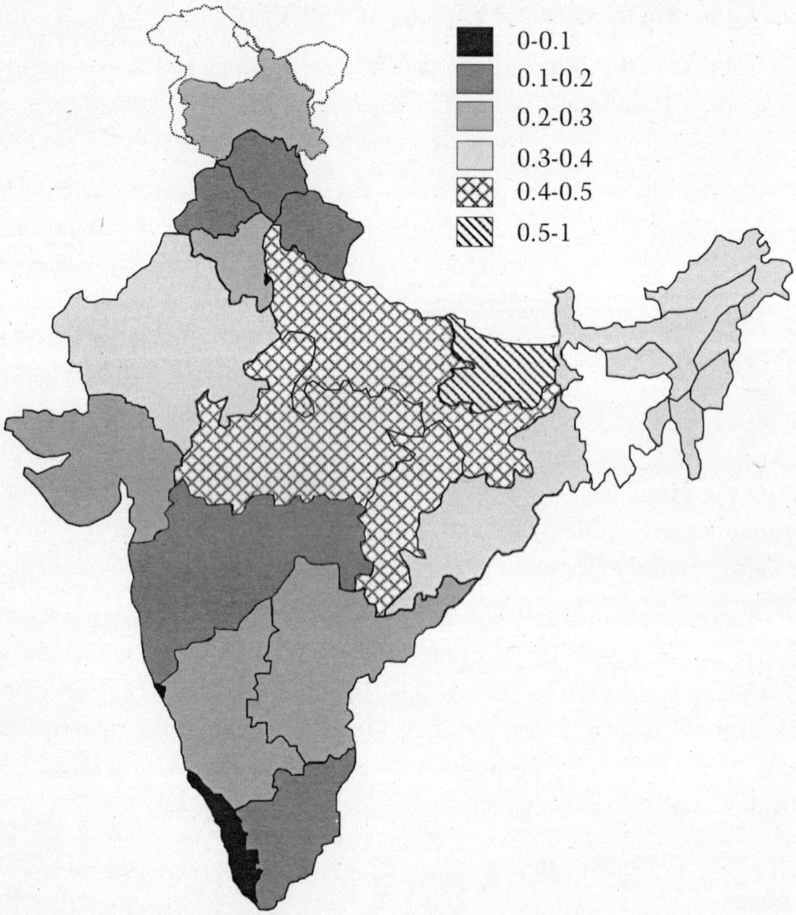

Source: Alkire and Santos (2010).

Table 2.1

Multidimensional Poverty across Indian States

MPI Rank	*States*	*Population in 2007 (million)*	*MPI*	*Proportion of Poor (%)*	*Average Intensity (%)*	*Contribution to Overall Poverty (%)*	*No. of MPI Poor (million)*
1	Kerala	35.0	0.065	15.90	40.90	0.60	5.6
2	Goa	1.6	0.094	21.70	43.40	0.00	0.4
3	Punjab	27.1	0.12	26.20	46.00	1.00	7.1
4	Himachal Pradesh	6.7	0.131	31.00	42.30	0.30	2.1
5	Tamil Nadu	68.0	0.141	32.40	43.60	2.60	22.0
6	Uttarakhand	9.6	0.189	40.30	46.90	0.50	3.9
7	Maharashtra	108.7	0.193	40.10	48.10	6.00	43.6
8	Haryana	24.1	0.199	41.60	47.90	1.30	10.0
9	Gujarat	57.3	0.205	41.50	49.20	3.40	23.8
10	Jammu and Kashmir	12.2	0.209	43.80	47.70	0.70	5.4
11	Andhra Pradesh	83.9	0.211	44.70	47.10	5.10	37.5
12	Karnataka	58.6	0.223	46.10	48.30	4.20	27.0
13	Eastern Indian States (4)	44.2	0.303	57.60	52.50	4.00	25.5
14	West Bengal	89.5	0.317	58.30	54.30	8.50	52.2
15	Orissa	40.7	0.345	64.00	54.00	4.30	26.0
16	Rajasthan	65.4	0.351	64.20	54.70	7.00	41.9
17	Uttar Pradesh	192.6	0.386	69.90	55.20	21.30	134.7
18	Chhattisgarh	23.9	0.387	71.90	53.90	2.90	17.2
19	Madhya Pradesh	70.0	0.389	69.50	56.00	8.50	48.6
20	Jharkhand	30.5	0.463	77.00	60.20	4.20	23.5
21	Bihar	95.0	0.499	81.40	61.30	13.50	77.3
	India	**1,164.70**	**0.296**	**55.40**	**53.50**	**-**	**645**

Source: OPHI (2010).

A decomposition of MPI in terms of its individual components shows that the deprivation is not only deep but it is all pervasive. This seems to suggest that the population of Bihar does not enjoy any of the benefits associated with rural living, but suffers from all the disadvantages that citizens in rural areas normally experience in terms of assets, amenities and services.

The cluster on standard of living accounts for the largest share in overall deprivation (i.e., 39.0%). While indicators under this cluster are built around the house which is individually owned, they also reflect the characteristics of the habitat (e.g. a *basti* of the SC community which is typically deprived of services and amenities such as electricity connection).

Table 2.2

Acute Multidimensional Poverty across States

States	Proportion of People who are Deprived in									
	Education		Health		Standard of Living					
	Schooling	Child Enrollment	Mortality	Nutrition	Electricity	Sanitation	Drinking Water	Floor	Cooking Fuel	Assets
Delhi	0.04	0.09	0.07	0.09	0	0.10	0.03	0.02	0.05	0.06
Kerala	0.01	0.07	0.04	0.12	0.05	0.04	0.09	0.03	0.15	0.11
Goa	0.04	0.09	0.04	0.16	0.02	0.16	0.10	0.12	0.17	0.12
Punjab	0.08	0.13	0.09	0.17	0.02	0.20	0.01	0.16	0.23	0.11
Himachal Pradesh	0.04	0.07	0.09	0.25	0.01	0.28	0.08	0.15	0.29	0.20
Tamil Nadu	0.09	0.08	0.11	0.21	0.07	0.31	0.05	0.12	0.30	0.24
Uttarakhand	0.08	0.10	0.15	0.30	0.15	0.33	0.10	0.30	0.37	0.27
Maharashtra	0.08	0.15	0.14	0.30	0.13	0.36	0.08	0.27	0.34	0.28
Haryana	0.08	0.20	0.15	0.30	0.08	0.34	0.08	0.24	0.39	0.25
Gujarat	0.12	0.13	0.17	0.33	0.09	0.36	0.10	0.24	0.36	0.29
Jammu & Kashmir	0.08	0.22	0.16	0.27	0.05	0.40	0.17	0.28	0.39	0.27
Andhra Pradesh	0.19	0.13	0.16	0.29	0.08	0.41	0.06	0.19	0.42	0.35
Karnataka	0.12	0.21	0.17	0.33	0.08	0.41	0.12	0.19	0.42	0.32
Eastern Indian States	0.19	0.21	0.19	0.37	0.41	0.45	0.23	0.50	0.55	0.42
West Bengal	0.25	0.23	0.19	0.42	0.41	0.47	0.07	0.48	0.57	0.43
Orissa	0.23	0.19	0.24	0.45	0.43	0.62	0.20	0.51	0.63	0.49
Rajasthan	0.21	0.32	0.28	0.44	0.31	0.60	0.24	0.36	0.61	0.47
Uttar Pradesh	0.18	0.36	0.37	0.46	0.48	0.62	0.07	0.58	0.66	0.41
Chhattisgarh	0.21	0.29	0.31	0.52	0.24	0.69	0.22	0.64	0.70	0.48
Madhya Pradesh	0.22	0.32	0.31	0.50	0.25	0.65	0.31	0.57	0.67	0.52
Jharkhand	0.26	0.45	0.30	0.56	0.55	0.73	0.42	0.63	0.76	0.55
Bihar	0.35	0.52	0.35	0.61	0.65	0.74	0.04	0.70	0.79	0.57
India	0.18	0.25	0.23	0.39	0.29	0.49	0.12	0.40	0.38	0.38

Source: Alkire and Santos (2010).

Recent NSS data also throws light on the structure of deprivation with regard to house and amenities. It shows that as many as 23.1 per cent of the rural households in Bihar live in 'unserviceable *katcha* houses' as compared to 5.0 per cent at the all-India level. Nearly 80 per cent of the households do not have a latrine as against the all-India figure of 65 per cent. Barely a quarter of the households have access to electricity for domestic use as against the figure of two-thirds at the all-India level (NSS, 2009). A recent Planning Commission-supported study by the Equity Foundation which carried out in-depth field survey in 12 blocks across four districts (*viz.*, Madhubani, Kishanganj, Vaishali and East Champaran) reports that electricity connection was present in just 6 per cent of the area (Equity Foundation, 2011).

Table 2.3

Distribution (per 1,000) of Households by Type of House Structure (State-wise)

State	*Type of Structure*					
			Katcha			
	Pucca	*Semi-Pucca*	*Katcha*	*Unserviceable Katcha*	*All Katcha*	*All*
Andhra Pradesh	702	162	92	44	136	1000
Bihar	445	200	123	231	355	1000
Gujarat	623	292	79	7	85	1000
Haryana	929	49	21	1	22	1000
Karnataka	483	451	53	14	66	1000
Kerala	773	192	27	9	35	1000
Madhya Pradesh	465	475	51	9	60	1000
Maharashtra	656	299	31	14	45	1000
Orissa	328	266	388	19	406	1000
Punjab	904	64	31	2	32	1000
Rajasthan	653	193	122	32	154	1000
Tamil Nadu	610	203	157	29	186	1000
Uttar Pradesh	605	193	171	31	202	1000
West Bengal	363	385	212	41	253	1000
All-India	554	276	120	50	170	1000

Source: NSSO (2009).

Micro-studies taking a deeper look at the ground-level realities present an even more alarming picture. A recent study on migration from

Samastipur in Bihar to Delhi found that in the sample villages at the point of origin, 40.8 per cent of the SC households did not have legal rights or documents for their house (Bhaskaran and Mehta, 2010).

Box 2.1

Housing and Sanitation in Rural Samastipur

Majority of the respondents (83.6%) reported having proper legal rights over their houses. Rest of them (14.4%) did not have any ownership rights over their houses as they were either living in rental houses or on public land.

Community-wise analysis shows that 40.8 per cent of the SC households did not have legal right or documents for their house.

Only 33 per cent of the households had semi-*pucca* or *pucca* houses. Majority of the SC households (81.6%) had thatched/*khaprail* houses.

Only 10 per cent of the sample households reported having toilet facility and majority (90%) still resorted to open defecation.

There was hardly any awareness among the villagers of the Total Sanitation Campaign (TSC). However, some migrants, who had come back on a holiday, informed that they were planning to construct a public well as well as toilet in their hamlet.

'If basic infrastructure and facilities like regular electricity supply, better irrigation and transportation are improved, the village would be able to absorb their new found skills for the development of on-farm and off-farm activities. At present the development status of the origin village is incapable of absorbing and utilising their skills and experiences in improving the village conditions and, hence, it may experience large scale outmigration in the coming days.'

Source: Bhaskaran and Mehta (2010).

This study concludes that the (poor) development status of the origin villages may trigger 'large scale outmigration in the coming days'. Other specific responses in this study reinforce this conclusion. This is discussed in more depth in Chapter 5 on migration.

The NSS data shows that proportionately much large number of households in Bihar is undertaking construction activities. But the cost of construction per household in Bihar is Rs 7,000 as against Rs 32,000 at the all-India level. Thus, these activities appear to be small maintenance-type activities by poor households and perhaps show the sorry state of the current assets.

Table 2.4

Distribution (per 1,000) of Households by Type of House Structure (State-wise)

State	*Proportion (per 1,000) of Households who undertook Constructions*	*Average Number of Constructions per Household*	*Average Cost (Rs '000) per Construction*
Andhra Pradesh	122	1.01	69
Bihar	172	1	7
Gujarat	74	1.04	51
Haryana	65	1	97
Karnataka	47	1.02	84
Kerala	151	1.07	128
Madhya Pradesh	58	1.01	25
Maharashtra	84	1.01	34
Orissa	53	1.01	51
Punjab	62	1.03	102
Rajasthan	69	1.01	54
Tamil Nadu	57	1.01	51
Uttar Pradesh	124	1.02	15
West Bengal	244	1.03	11
All-India	120	1.02	32

Source: NSSO (2009).

The report of the Equity Foundation (2011) concludes, 'homelessness and the dilapidated condition of houses in the rural sites were also identified as major problems by the respondents in almost all the areas covered under study. Repairing houses was a major expenditure head for the poor households, and every alternate year, a significant amount of money had to be spent in bringing houses to livable conditions. Indira Awaas Yojna (IAY) was found to be a total failure in almost all the villages covered in the study as it was distributed among the privileged class people'.

The above baseline shows that deprivation is most severe in terms of the basic assets—the house and connected amenities. Thus, the remedial measures must strengthen this asset base of the individual households. At the same time, such 'asset creation/enrichment' cannot be effectively addressed at the level of individual households. A habitat-wide approach will be necessary. The available evidence on high social stratification and economic inequities in the villages as well as feedback from the migrant population on the conditions required at the point of origin (discussed in Chapter 5) suggest the need for opening up new habitat options. It appears that opportunity for safe and secure mobility might be of considerable value to the vulnerable sections in accessing services and assets from government programmes and in starting on a new path.

The Navodaya Shahar model seeks to provide this option in a manner that is not disruptive in terms of the occupational characteristics, geographical location or the social moorings. This is discussed in more depth in Chapter 6 on the Navodaya Shahar model.

2.3 The Land Question

The Bihar Rural Livelihoods Promotion Society (2007) notes, 'India's rural economy in general and that of Bihar in particular, are entirely dependent on land and agricultural activities...landless and land-poor households, therefore, constitute the large bulk of "below poverty line" households throughout the country. According to one estimate, nearly 70 per cent of the landless wage earners and nearly 45 per cent of the marginal farmer households in India live below poverty line (NCAER, 1996)'.

The World Bank (2005) states, 'in fact, 75 per cent of the rural poor in Bihar were landless or near landless in 1999-2000. This expanded by eight per cent since 1993-94...the high levels of inequality that have persisted in land ownership may be partly attributed to slack progress in land reform in the state.' The report concludes, 'reducing rural poverty in Bihar means providing security of tenure to small and marginal farmers and the landless through effective implementation of land reforms.'

Data from NSS 64th Round (July 2007-June 08) presents the following picture in respect of land distribution across states. It is clear that more than 60 per cent of the rural population in Bihar is landless or has land less than 0.20 hectares. Considering the high dependence of the rural population in Bihar on land-based livelihood, this land distribution pattern reflects the scenario of poverty in masses. This data, however, does not capture the concentration of land across different segments.

Table 2.5

Distribution of Rural Households by the Size Class of Land Possessed (State-wise)

States	*Per 1,000 Number of Households possessing Land of Size (ha)*									
	Upto 0.01	*0.02-0.20*	*0.21-0.40*	*0.41-1.00*	*1.01-2.00*	*2.01-3.00*	*3.01-4.00*	*4.01-6.00*	*> 6.01*	*Total*
Andhra Pradesh	502	97	84	141	108	43	8	12	6	1000
Bihar	337	263	132	174	62	22	8	2	1	1000
Gujarat	390	112	102	168	122	50	17	20	18	1000
Haryana	417	142	54	135	118	62	24	25	24	1000
Karnataka	392	88	72	205	153	50	14	12	14	1000
Kerala	176	555	135	87	37	6	1	1	1	1000
Madhya Pradesh	260	98	104	153	226	69	40	24	27	1000
Maharashtra	415	87	74	134	152	55	25	32	26	1000
Orissa	258	185	200	221	106	19	6	4	2	1000
Punjab	464	180	64	88	87	56	11	25	25	1000
Rajasthan	154	78	123	252	225	67	24	31	45	1000
Tamil Nadu	571	171	89	103	46	13	4	2	1	1000
Uttar Pradesh	287	170	162	223	104	33	10	7	5	1000
West Bengal	491	261	109	106	25	6	1	1	0	1000
All-India	346	172	121	177	114	35	13	11	10	1000

Source: NSSO (2010a).

Data from NSS 64th Round (July 2007-June 08) also shows that the share of 'agriculture labour' in Bihar is significantly higher than the all-India average. The share of 'other labour households' in the state is much lower as compared to the all-India average (Table 2.6). This indicates that Bihar is behind the curve in terms of workforce transition.

Table 2.6

Distribution of Rural Households (per 1,000) by Household Type (State-wise)

States	Self-Employed in Agriculture	Self-Employed in Non-Agriculture	Self-Employed in All	Agriculture Labour Households	Other Labour Households	Others	Total
Andhra Pradesh	229	145	374	367	98	161	1000
Bihar	325	161	486	367	42	104	1000
Gujarat	369	119	488	281	119	112	1000
Haryana	403	144	547	120	180	153	1000
Karnataka	302	103	405	397	72	126	1000
Kerala	172	182	355	168	287	191	1000
Madhya Pradesh	460	79	539	333	64	63	1000
Maharashtra	316	107	423	347	104	126	1000
Orissa	311	168	478	297	92	133	1000
Punjab	280	144	424	191	179	206	1000
Rajasthan	495	124	619	80	191	110	1000
Tamil	185	134	318	347	211	123	1000
Uttar Pradesh	480	153	632	166	95	107	1000
West Bengal	202	222	424	352	112	111	1000
All-India	350	144	494	266	115	125	1000

Source: NSSO (2010b).

There is a strong link between social identity, landlessness and poverty across the country. But this link is much more strongly entrenched in the case of Bihar.

Table 2.7

Percentage of Population, Mean Consumption and Land Ownership by Social Class (Rural)

	50th Round (1993-94)			55th Round (1999-2000)		
	% of Population	Median PC Expenditure	Median Land Owned (ha)	% of Population	Median PC Expenditure	Median Land Owned (ha)
Majority	70	206	0.42	72	368	0.25
SC/ST	30	175	0.04	28	312	0.03
Total	100	197	0.35	100	349	0.2

Note: PC – Per Capita.

Source: The World Bank (2005).

D. Bandyopadhyay who headed the Bihar Land Reforms Commission concludes, 'the landownership pattern in Bihar remains acutely skewed even now. The National Sample Survey Organisation's (NSSO) Survey Report No. 491, 2003, on landholding patterns reveals a disquieting picture. Marginal and small farmers who constituted 96.5 per cent of the total landowning community owned 66 per cent of land. Medium and large farmers who constituted only 3.5 per cent of the total landowning community owned 33 per cent of the land. Of the latter, the large owners (constituting only 0.1 per cent of the total) own 4.63 per cent of total land. In absolute terms, this 0.1 per cent of the large owners owned a little over 8 lakh hectares or 19.76 lakh acres of land—a colossal amount by Indian standards. Such a high concentration of landholding in the hands of a minuscule number of owners and with archaic production relations is a major roadblock against increased production and productivity in agriculture in Bihar' (Bandyopadhyay, 2009).

Land Reforms in Bihar

Bihar was the first state in independent India to legislate on land reforms. The Bihar Abolition of Zamindari Act, 1948 sought to eliminate the intermediaries between the actual tillers and the state. As this Act was challenged in the court, follow-up legislations were brought in.

To redress the iniquitous distribution of land that continued despite the above legislative measures, the Bihar Land Ceiling Act, 1961 was passed. There were subsequent amendments in 1972 and 1973. Legislative measures in land reforms also sought to safeguard the interests of the tenants through security of tenure and fixation of rent. Other relevant legislations included the Bihar Privileged Persons Homestead Tenancy Act (1947) and the Bihar Moneylenders Act (1974).

These legislations, however, could not provide the desired breakthrough due to a lack of political will, resistance from the landed sections and connivance of the bureaucracy. Large-scale violations of the Ceiling Act through *'benami'* transfer of land and wrong classification of land and areas to minimise the extent of surplus land were reported. The state government was also highly tentative and tardy in taking measures to acquire whatever land that was declared surplus. For example, landowners who were declared as retaining ceiling-surplus land as on 19 April 1962 were served notices in 1970. In the first phase, notices were served only to 125 landowners (Sharma, 2009).

Reportedly, whereas the surplus land amounted to 20.51 per cent of the total land mass in Bihar, only 1.53 per cent of the cultivable land was acquired and distributed. As of January 2001, the ceiling process accumulated 3.85 lakh acres. Almost a quarter of the land assessed as surplus by the government was left to the owners on various grounds. Landowners again took resort to filing cases and about 1 lakh acre is under litigation. Thus, only 2.77 lakh acres was distributed among 3.52 lakh families. 'Other castes' constituted 48 per cent of the beneficiaries and received 38 per cent of the total area allotted. The landless SCs and STs community which had the main claim for land were deprived to this extent (Sharma, 2009). Sharma adds, 'The average extent of land allotted was less than one acre, which is not economically viable. Those who were allotted uncultivable land were miserable. The facilities of irrigation, lending and rural development scheme were not well integrated with the allotments.'

Reports indicate that the distribution of government land was comparatively higher than the ceiling land distributed.

The 'Bhoodan' movement led by Acharya Vinoba Bhave has been central to the issue of surplus land for redistribution to the landless. But it appears to have taken a curious turn overtime. An interim report of the Bihar Land Reforms Commission issued on June 4, 2007 throws light on the rather bewildering state of affairs. The report notes, 'the most astounding feature...was that 11,130.9375 acres were distributed among 59 institutions. The categorisation of "Common and Others" is totally vague and confusing. From the analysis it is apparent that someone is utilising the Bhoodan land as his or her private zamindari. The report also shows that about 15000 acres have not yet been distributed formally. No one knows whether some person or a body of persons is/are utilising such huge area for their private gain...there is another problem regarding the figures maintained by the Committee and that maintained by the Revenue Department. According to Revenue Department figures land not so far confirmed is around 1,11,000 acres. According to the figures maintained by the Committee, there is no reliable figure of land not so far confirmed. This anomaly is a major source of local disputes and trouble.' The Commission prescribed a time-bound programme to reconcile the above discrepancies based on physical survey and verification of land (LRC, 2007).

A study by Ekta Parishad and Praxis, which are leading land rights movement, considers that Bihar accounted for more than 50 per cent of the total of 21.16 lakh acres gifted during the 'Bhoodan' movement in the country and that some 3.97 lakh acres remains to be distributed (Ekta Parishad and Praxis, 2009). This study also indicates that a large proportion of households that were distributed—ceiling surplus land, 'Bhoodan' land, homestead plots etc., were not able to gain control of such assets.

Tenancy is another important aspect of the agrarian baseline in Bihar. 'The tenants are usually labourers, poor peasants and marginal farmers, but small cultivators have also started leasing in land. Many researchers have highlighted the interlinkage between iniquitous landholding pattern, sharecropping, economic stagnation in the countryside and immiseration of the poor' (Sharma, 2009). Various studies indicate that tenancy is rampant and covers as much as a third of the agricultural land in Bihar. (Bandyopadhyay, 2009 and Sharma, 2009).

The Bihar Land Reforms Commission (2006-2008)

Soon upon assuming power, the Chief Minster, Nitish Kumar sought to revive the initiative in land reforms. He set up the Bihar Land Reforms Commission (LRC) in 2006 under the leadership of D. Bandyopadhyay (IAS retd.), one of the key architects of land reforms in West Bengal.

The Commission submitted its report in 2008. 'The three main recommendations are: (i) to do away with the present system of classification of land into six categories with varying ceilings over 15 acres; (ii) to allot between 1 acre and 0.66 acre of ceiling surplus land to the lowest quintile of agricultural labourers consisting of 16.68 lakh households each and assignment of at least 10 decimals of land to shelter-less households of 5.48 lakh non-farm rural workers each, and (iii) to enact a Bataidari Act to ensure secure and heritable right of cultivation to all tenants/sharecroppers with 60 per cent share of the produce (if the landowner bears the cost of production) or 70 to 75 per cent of the produce (if the *bataidar* bears the cost of production)' (Mainstream, 2009).

Box 2.2

Mainstream: Implement Bandyopadhyay Commission's Recommendations for Land Reforms

'Land reforms are central to any real battle against Bihar's backwardness. With 90 per cent of the state's population living in villages and 74 per cent workforce employed in agriculture, Bihar is still predominantly rural or agrarian. Yet agriculture accounts for only 33 per cent of the state's domestic product and the landholding pattern remains absolutely skewed. Marginal and small farmers constituting roughly 96.5 per cent of total landowners own about 66 per cent of the total land while medium and large farmers constituting only 3.5 per cent of the landowning community own roughly 33 per cent of the total land. Citing NSSO figures, the LRC report points to a reverse trend of land concentration: between 1992 and 2003, the proportion of large landowners has gone down from 0.2 per cent to 0.1 per cent, yet their share in total land area has increased from 4.44 per cent to 4.63 per cent over the same period!

The proportion of the landless or the near landless among the rural poor is steadily increasing—from 67 per cent in 1993-94 to 75 per cent by the turn of the century. Between 1991 and 2001, outmigration from Bihar increased by over 200 per cent, whereas the average increase for all the Indian states stood at just 21.5 per cent. Landlessness aggravates poverty and forces people to migrate out of the state; landlessness also retards the development of agriculture. Between 1991-92 and 1995-96, agriculture in Bihar grew at the negative rate of (-) 2 per cent annum, followed by a very sluggish 0.8 per cent of annual recovery for the next six years (when nationally agriculture grew at three per cent per annum). If despite having 'perhaps the most fertile soil in the world and copious water resources' agricultural growth remains so sluggish in Bihar, the LRC finds it 'evident that there is a structural bottleneck in Bihar agriculture due to a very queer pattern of land ownership and very extortionate system of tenancy at will which are causing great impediment to accelerated rate of agricultural growth.'

The LRC sees land reforms as the key to reforming the relations of agricultural production and releasing 'the forces of production dormant in the economy, which would propel the development of the State'. 'As a predominantly agricultural State, Bihar would have no option but to take to effective land reforms to burst asunder the fetters and shackles which had been preventing its many splendoured advancement,' urges the LRC report.'

Source: Mainstream (2009).

These recommendations have run into heavy political headwinds and are reportedly in 'cold storage'. Various movements for land rights are however, actively pressing for the implementation of the LRC recommendations, and particularly for distribution of the 'Bhoodan' land.

Although the LRC report has been put in cold storage, the Bihar government is moving on in distribution of surplus land. Quoting an official of the Chief Minister's office, a recent newspaper report indicates that the state government has distributed over 14,000 acres of land among the 30,000 poor and landless women between 2007 and 2010. These are all 'Bhoodan' lands. The *Bihar Economic Survey* presents the following overview on distribution of various categories of land.

Figure 2.4

Overview of Distribution of Land in Bihar

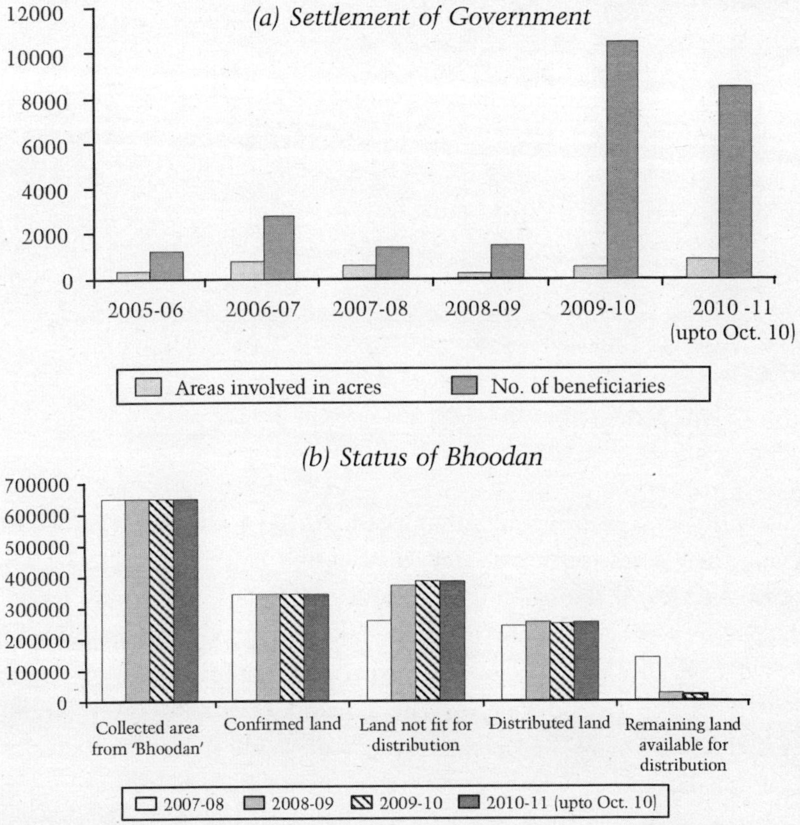

(c) Settlement of Sariat

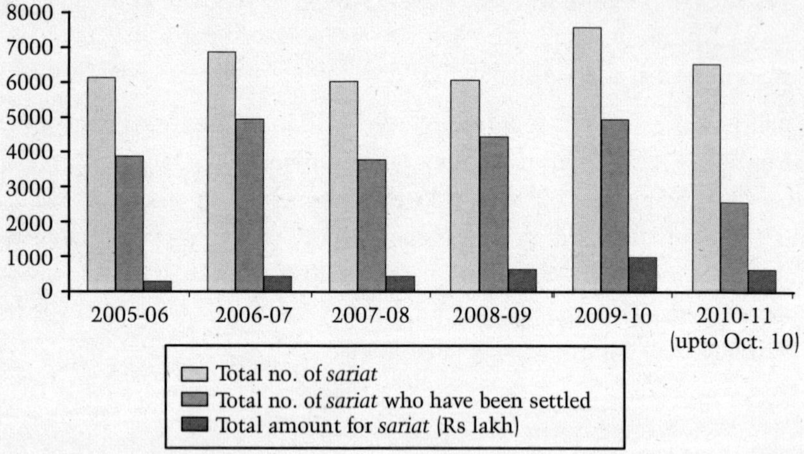

(d) Distribution of Homestead Land

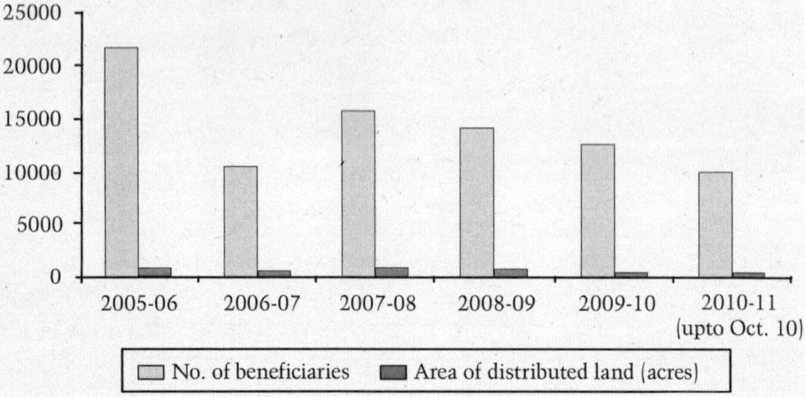

Source: *Bihar Economic Survey 2010-11*, Government of Bihar.

Overall, land reforms in Bihar seem to have failed miserably in achieving their objective of equitable distribution of this key asset. They have also tied down the agricultural sector to dismal productivity levels. Bandyopadhyay concludes, 'In the first half of the 1990s agriculture in Bihar had a negative growth rate of (–) 2 per cent per year. Later, up to the early part of the first decade of the present century it grew at an imperceptible rate of (+) 0.8 per cent per year. With all the technologies available in the market why is it that the actual tillers are not accessing them. It is evident that there is a structural bottleneck in Bihar agriculture due to very queer pattern of land ownership and very extortion-ate system of tenancy-at-will which are causing great impediment to accelerated rate of agricultural growth' (*Report of the Bihar Land Reforms Commission*, p .4) (Bandyopadhyay, 2009).

While most scholars agree with the above diagnosis, some of the recent influential studies and policy research initiatives part ways with Bandyopadhyay in so far as future strategies are concerned.

The Steering Group on Vision of Agriculture Development in Bihar concludes, '...these holdings are fragmented in a large number of parcels. With an average size of holdings of 0.60 ha. there are, on an average, 3.3 parcels per holding. These holdings do not receive the benefits of various facilities such as subsidised inputs, credit or extension services partly because of the high transaction cost but mainly because of the unhelpful attitude of various functionaries. Despite these handicaps the small farmers are able to hold on to their lands. Thus, graduating from marginal to small holdings and further to medium holdings, is a promising option, which can be achieved through the following measures:

- Legalising tenancy within the existing land ceiling provisions;
- Purchasing of land from landholders (who are willing to sell their lands) by the State Land Development and Finance Corporation and selling it to the small and marginal farmers at fair prices;
- Encouraging credit institutions to advance loans to marginal and small farmers to purchase land from various private and government sources;
- Encouraging large farmers to shift to non-agricultural enterprises;
- Distributing government surplus land in viable small holdings;
- Encouraging dairying, horticulture and vegetable growing, particularly on small and marginal farms;
- Promoting contract farming, and ensuring transparent and fair agreements between contracting parties;
- Encouraging the collective organisation of farmers with similar economic interests, and
- Drawing roadmap for consolidation of holdings, but should be done only after creating suitable environment for its implementation and proper training of the officials engaged in land administration.

The precondition for fair and just land reforms is reliable land records, which can be formulated through GPS technology and computerisation' (GoB, 2010).

The above recommendation of the Steering Group breathes in three new strands. First, it prefers the less disruptive route of making overt the institutional arrangements that are omnipotent but lurk in shadows. Second, it talks of the relevance of market-based interventions in a pro-poor reform context. Third, it brings in a certain dynamic perspective as against the traditional land reforms paradigm which looks at distribution of land as a one-time measure.

The recommendations of the Steering Group open up a new direction. But it is important to note that given the preponderance of agriculture in the livelihoods of the rural masses, transformation in this sector is not a sectoral agenda. An all encompassing change that covers other aspects such as the habitat structure and the human development baseline is required. Thus, there is a need to go much further without losing the original objective of land reforms. In this context, the concluding sub-section in this Chapter outlines the concept of 'land reforms plus'.

2.4 The Education Sector

Studies under OPHI using NFHS 3 data (2005-06) show that education accounts for as much as 29 per cent of the overall MPI deprivation in Bihar. The corresponding all-India average is 24.0 per cent. However, a comparison in terms of the proportion of people deprived in the education-related indicators shows that 35 per cent of Bihar's population was deprived in terms of schooling as compared to 1 per cent in Kerala, 19 per cent in Andhra Pradesh and 18 per cent in the neighbouring state of Uttar Pradesh. In terms of child school attendance, the picture was even more alarming. As high as 52 per cent of Bihar's population was deprived in terms of this indicator as compared to 7 per cent in Kerala, 13 per cent in Andhra Pradesh and 36 per cent in Uttar Pradesh (Alkire and Santos, 2010).

Recent Trends in Education

The recent trend, however, shows a sharp take-off from the above dismal baseline. The 2011 Census captures this spectacular progress.

Between 2001 and 2011, the state recorded a jump of 74.83 per cent in the number of literates. A comparison across the Empowered Action Group (EAG) states shows that Bihar's achievement was nearly twice that of states such as Orissa and Madhya Pradesh (Census, 2011). But there is a long road ahead—Bihar with a literacy rate of 63.82 per cent in 2011 still stands at the bottom of the list of states.

As per the *Bihar Economic Survey 2010-11*, the enrollment of boys at the primary level increased at an annual growth rate of 7.67 per cent between 2002-2009. For girls, the growth rate was 6.92 per cent per annum. A major transformation came at the upper primary level. The overall enrollment at the upper primary level for all boys increased at an annual growth rate of 20.47 per cent in this period. The rate for SC boys was at 24.05 per cent per annum while that for ST boys it was 27.20 per cent per annum. For all girls, the enrollment in upper primary has been growing at 26.64 per cent annually. For SC girls, the growth rate was 31.73 per cent per annum and for ST girls the rate was 33.46 per cent per annum.

The dropout rates at the primary and upper primary levels also declined sharply during 2001-02 to 2008-09. At the primary education level, it declined by 16.6 percentage points and the decline was higher in the case of girls, as compared to boys.

The impressive performance in terms of enrollment and drop-out rates is the result of doubling of the school capacity at the upper primary level and measures such as universalisation of the mid-day meal scheme (MDMS) to all primary schools, including learning centres in 2005—the total coverage by 2009-10 was 79.9 per cent, up from 75.7 per cent in 2008-09.

Table 2.8

Availability of Schools in Relation to Population

Indicators	*2002*	*2009*
1) No. of primary and upper primary schools/10,000 population	6.05	6.98
a) No. of primary schools/10,000 population	4.88	4.68
b) No. of upper primary schools/10,000 population	1.17	2.29
2) No. of secondary and senior secondary schools/10,000 population	0.41	0.41
a) No. of secondary schools/10,000 population	0.37	0.28
b) No. of senior secondary schools/10,000 population	0.04	0.13

Source: *Bihar Economic Survey 2010-11*, Government of Bihar.

The state government has succeeded in changing the baseline in so far as primary and upper primary education is concerned. But this consumed around 60 per cent of the sectoral budget. Also, as the following analysis suggests, certain major areas of concern stand out. These will require structural solutions.

First, there is significant inter-district disparity in availability of school infrastructure, in literacy rates as well enrollment and dropout rates. According to the *Bihar Economic Survey 2010-11*, the spurt in enrollment is concentrated in 15 districts of Bihar, while another 16 districts are lagging behind. More districts are lagging behind in the process of accelerated enrollment of SC students compared to the rate of growth of overall enrollment. Similarly, under MDMS, there is high variation across districts. There is more than 95 per cent coverage in Munger, Lakhisarai and Sheikhpura. But the coverage is below 50 per cent in Banka (19.63%), Madhubani (34.30%), and Bhagalpur (46.45%).

Second, the rate of decline in dropout rates at the primary and upper primary levels began to decelerate in the latter part of the last decade.

Third, in the area of secondary education, there has been no improvement in infrastructure and the dropout rates at this level remain uniformly and significantly high for all social groups—above 80 per cent for the general category students, above 85 per cent for ST students and above 90 per cent for SC students. Sooner than later, such conditions are likely to affect the motivation levels in the lower classes and undo some of gains made at that level.

The report of the Equity Foundation referred to above indicates that 50 per cent of the respondents reported presence of either government primary schools, private schools or *aanganwadi* centres in their villages. 'However, education from secondary level onwards in most of the villages surveyed seemed to be the missing link. The distance of nearest Secondary school and high schools and Colleges vary from 10 to 25 kms. School infrastructure up to middle level is available in more villages compared to secondary schools. According to the respondents they were not aware about any college in their area. Hence illiteracy is a big hindrance in the development of human capital and lack of skilled labour force participation apart from having implications for individual welfare and economic growth' (Equity Foundation, 2011).

Now, while a breakthrough in primary education may have been possible by making the village-level primary schools functional, a much larger and more organised infrastructure will be required for boosting secondary and senior secondary education. Such schools will cover a number of villages. But as the Equity Foundation's report concludes, 'lack of transport facilities, particularly in rural areas for girls to attend middle and secondary schools, which are sufficiently far away from their habitations, is one of the major causes of the large-scale dropout of girls after completing lower primary'. Thus suitable infrastructure in terms of hostels etc., may be required. Also, the problem of senior teachers shifting base to villages is well known. Thus, again improving secondary and senior secondary education will necessitate a network of intermediate habitats.

Such habitats will also help attract private entrepreneurs to set up good quality and accredited schools, especially at the secondary and senior secondary level—a measure that is much needed in view of the paucity in public resources.

Box 2.3

The Beautiful Tree

It is widely held that the poor communities are served mainly by public schools. It is also believed that private schools which have come up in poor communities are dispensing low quality education, but at a much higher fee. As such, the demand for tight regulation of such schools is very strong.

In his recent book, 'The Beautiful Tree', Prof. Tooley presents evidence to demolish such received development wisdom. He concludes:

- There are large numbers of private schools in developing countries, and in some places these educate more children from poor families than do Government schools.
- These schools serve the poor by charging minimal fees—$10 per year in some cases, and generally in the range 4-20 per cent of the minimum wage. In addition, they offer free education to a few deserving cases. These private schools operate in a highly competitive environment. The salaries in such private schools are

contd...

...contd...

> much lower than in highly unionised public schools. Considering the hidden costs in Government schools by way of uniforms etc., the costs in private schools compare well with those in public schools.

The results of the tests administered by Tooley and his team on 24,000 children in India, Nigeria, Ghana and China, in Maths and language proficiency may come as a surprise to many. In India and Africa, in almost all respects, the children in private schools performed better than those in Government schools. Only in provision of playgrounds did the Government schools do better.

In Africa and India, the existence of private schools seems to be, at least partly, a function of perceived shortcomings in Government provision. In China, however, they cater mainly for children in remote rural villages as parents are reluctant to send their children (especially their daughters) to distant Government schools.

The entrepreneurs generally value their status in the local community. They are in no position to exploit parents, as they are often accused of doing. Private schools seem to be compensating in various ways for their less qualified teachers and poor school infrastructure because they are directly accountable. On the other hand, there is often a lack of accountability of teachers in Government schools.

Poor parents are making an informed choice in sending their children to such schools. They are also doing all they can to ensure quality. On the other hand, government inspectors of schools in many countries are under-resourced and potentially seeking 'unofficial payments' rather than enforcing the rules.

Prof. Tooley stresses on the need to find those private sector providers, often based in the poorest areas and to devise activities to support them in a manner that makes sense both to them and to the larger development scenario.

Source: Tooley (2009).

2.5. The Health Sector

The MPI discussion above shows that the baseline of the health sector in Bihar entails a similar high order of deprivation. For example, 35 per cent of Bihar's population is shown as deprived in terms of the mortality indicator as compared to 4 per cent in Kerala and 16 per cent in Andhra Pradesh. In this indicator, UP falls in the same bracket as Bihar.

Recent Trends

In the recent past, however, Bihar has seen a steady improvement in health indicators. There has been a rapid expansion in vaccination coverage and the rural-urban gap in this indicator has disappeared. According to the, Sample Registration System (SRS) Bulletin issued by the Registrar General of India in January 2011, the Infant Mortality Rate (IMR) in Bihar declined to 52 in 2009 and was close to the all India figure of 50. The antenatal care, however, saw a slower pace of change with more responsiveness observed in urban areas.

There has been a sharp increase in number of patients visiting government facilities for health care.

Table 2.9

Number of Patients Visiting Government Hospitals

Month	*2006*	*2007*	*2008*	*2009*	*2010*
January	39	2243	2522	1597	3526
February	653	2224	2693	3161	4288
March	1018	2257	2778	4264	4841
April	1101	2120	2825	3595	4674
May	1306	2784	3908	3155	4957
June	1547	3508	3900	3875	5069
July	2758	4093	4905	4538	5857
August	3063	3851	4817	4591	5874
September	2685	4140	5521	4280	4406
October	2454	4513	4505	3991	4768
November	2638	3188	3884	4819	
December	2565	1998	4000	4042	

Source: *Bihar Economic Survey 2010-11*, Government of Bihar.

However, as in the education sector, a number of structural bottlenecks are evident.

First, the state of reproductive health remains at a highly suboptimal level and displays large rural-urban disparity. For example, in rural areas 73.5 per cent of deliveries take place at home. Accordingly, only 29.5 per cent of the deliveries in rural areas are categorised as 'safe deliveries'. Similarly, in rural areas only 24.9 per cent of mothers received postnatal care within two weeks of delivery.

Table 2.10

Trend in Selected Health Indicators (2002-2004 to 2007-08)

Indicators	*DLHS III (2007-08)*			*DLHS II (2002-2004)*		
	Total	*Rural*	*Urban*	*Total*	*Rural*	*Urban*
Antenatal care						
Mothers who received any antenatal check-up (%)	59.3	58.5	70.8	31.4	31.3	58.9
Mothers who had antenatal check-up in first trimester (%)	24.2	22.9	40.7	18.5	16.3	38.4
Mothers who had three or more ANC (%)	26.4	25.4	39.8	16	13.8	36.2
Mothers who had full antenatal check-up (%)	4.6	4.0	11.7	4.3	3.4	12.4
Reproductive health						
Institutional delivery (%)	27.7	25.6	54.3	18.8	15.8	45.8
Delivery at home (%)	71.5	73.5	45.3	80.9	83.9	54.0
Safe delivery (%)	31.9	29.7	59.9	25.2	21.8	54.1
Mothers who received postnatal care within two weeks of delivery (%)	26.2	24.9	42.6	NA	NA	NA
Mothers who received financial assistance for delivery under JSY (%)	9.7	9.4	14.1	NA	NA	NA
Child immunisation						
Children 12-23 months fully immunised (%)	41.4	41.4	41.2	20.7	19.1	35.4
Children 12-23 months not received any vaccination (%)	1.6	1.5	2.7	51.8	53.5	36.2
Children 12-23 months who have received BCG vaccine (%)	81.5	81.6	80.4	44.6	42.6	62.2
Children 12-23 months who have received three doses of DPT vaccine (%)	54.4	54.5	53.8	31	29	49.1
Children 12-23 months who have received three doses of polio vaccine (%)	53.1	53	54	30.5	28.5	48.1
Children 12-23 months who have received measles vaccine (%)	54.2	54.1	55.8	24.4	22.7	40.1

Note: ANC - Antenatal Check-up
JSY - Janani Suraksha Yojana
BCG - Bacille Calmette Guerians
DPT - Diphtheria, Pertussis and Tetanus

Source: Bihar Economic Survey 2010-11, Government of Bihar.

Second, large inter-district variation in health infrastructure, coverage and outcome is evident.

Figure 2.5

District Level Coverage under JBSY

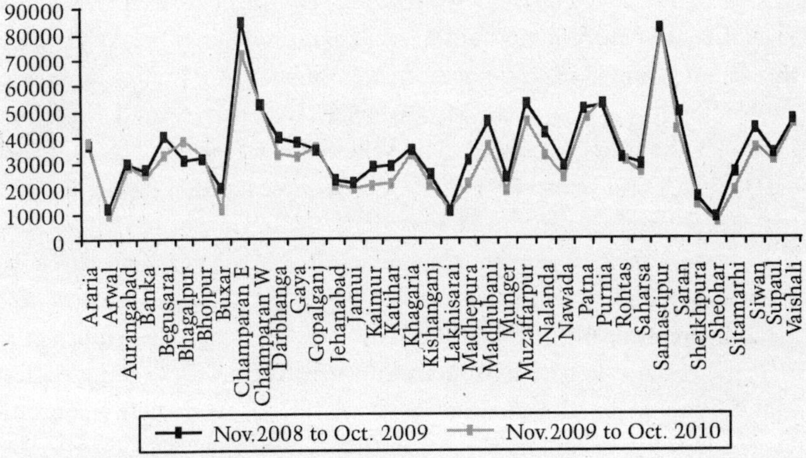

Note: JBSY - Janani Evam Bal Suraksha Yojana.

Source: Bihar Economic Survey 2010-11, Government of Bihar.

Figure 2.6

Construction of Hand Pumps under the Central Rural Water Supply Programme

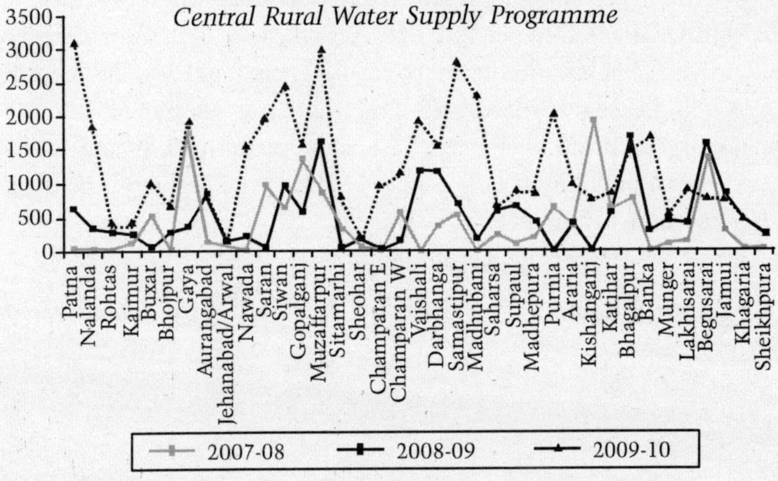

Source: Bihar Economic Survey 2010-11, Government of Bihar.

The study by the Equity Foundation referred to above found that 75 per cent of the women respondents (in the 12 blocks surveyed) spent 50 per cent to 70 per cent of their savings on the health-related problems of their family members. The study notes, 'Easily treatable diseases such as tuberculosis, poliomyelitis, leprosy, gastroenteritis and malaria are widespread. Many women die during childbirth due to a complete lack of maternity services. Because of poor or inadequate training, village doctors often fail to recognise life-threatening complications. The nearest hospital on an average in most of the blocks surveyed is over 10-20 km away; it is private and much too expensive for the people to afford. The spillover costs include higher service charges for drugs and transport, loss of income and education during times of illness, lower productivity, reducing income and output. PHSS existed according to less than 10 per cent respondents but they had no infrastructure and hence they had to go to the private doctors or "Quacks" (Ojha, Guni, Vaidya and Homoeopath)...For our present purpose it would be sufficient to say that the absence of bare minimum infrastructure on these counts places a negative impact on the positive participation of women in economic activities. It relegates them to a situation where their participation in economic activities is more driven by desperation and poverty rather than their skilled participation in economy' (Equity Foundation, 2011) .

Third, while the secular decline in health infrastructure from 2001 to 2006 was reversed between 2007 to 2009, this trend appears to be short-lived. The *Bihar Economic Survey 2010-11* notes, 'there were 10,632 health centres as on October 2010 as compared to 11,107 in December 2008. Of these, 494 are rural Primary Health Centres (PHCs), 37 are urban PHCs, 8,858 are health sub-centres and 1,243 are Additional PHCs. For every lakh of population, there were 11 health centres in 2009 and 2010, as compared to 13 in 2008. This is primarily due to the decline in number of sub-centres and urban PHCs in the last two years. There are wide variations in coverage at the district level.'

The shortfall in the rural health infrastructure across various categories is severe.

Table 2.11

Health Infrastructure Shortfall

Category	*Required*	*In-Position*	*Shortfall*
Sub-centre	14959	8858	6101
Primary health centre	2489	1774	715
Community health centre/referral hospitals	622	70	552
ANM	10499	9639	860

Note: ANM - Auxiliary Nurse Midwife.
Source: Bihar Economic Survey 2010-11, Government of Bihar.

Fourth, there has been a substantial increase in both the budget for the health sector and in the utilisation rate over 2005-06 to 2009-10. But this was from a very low base. Thus both these continue to be at sub-optimal levels.

Table 2.12

Overview of Public Expenditure in Health Sector

(Rs crore)

Year	*Approved Budget*	*Funds Received*		*Total Received*	*Total Expenditure*	*% Utilisation against Receipts*	*% Utilisation against Budget*
		GoI (NHRM)	*GoB*				
2005-06	398.22	124.33	-	124.33	38.62	31.1	9.7
2006-07	571.42	328.75	51.84	380.59	92.14	24.2	16.1
2007-08	680.7	240.2	175.37	415.57	237.8	57.2	34.9
2008-09	766.69	645.1	0.19	645.29	339.75	52.6	44.3
2009-10	1040.66	411.28	215.41	626.69	562.53	89.8	54.1
2010-11 (upto Oct.)	1029.15	271.63	95.72	367.35	273.83	74.5	26.6
Total	4486.84	2021.29	538.53	2559.82	1544.67	60.3	34.4

Note: GoI - Government of India.
GoB - Government of Bihar.
Source: Bihar Economic Survey 2010-11, Government of Bihar.

Thus again, creation of intermediate-level habitats will be of considerable value in energising the health sector. Particularly, as in the education sector, such habitats are likely to attract private entrepreneurs in setting up good quality and accredited dispensaries and hospitals. These agencies are likely to be more proactive in leveraging public health insurance schemes to create an organised health infrastructure for the poor.

2.6 Occupational Structure

The multidimensional deprivation discussed above is mirrored in a regressive occupational structure.

According to the Report of the Steering Group on Agriculture (GoB, 2010), 'agriculture contributes nearly 33 per cent to the state's GDP, but its share in the workforce is 74 per cent (as per 2008 figures). This asymmetry between the SGDP from agriculture and the workforce dependent on it has widened over a period of time, as employment opportunities in the non-farm sector in the rural areas have not increased.' Similarly, commenting on the effect of high dependence on the agricultural sector during the preceding two decades, the Report states, 'Bihar's economy started showing a decline in the late 1980s, and economic growth started decelerating in the next two decades. The only saving grace, however, has been the performance of agriculture. Between 1993 and 2003, the all-India agricultural GDP grew at 2.2 per cent per year. The corresponding figure for Bihar was 2.7 per cent. However, because of the overwhelming dependence of the state's workforce on agriculture, which was growing at the rate of 2.1 per cent per year, the increase in per capita income of the agricultural workers was only marginal.'

Table 2.6 above shows that the share of agriculture labour in Bihar is significantly higher than the all-India average while the share of other labour households in the state is lower.

Another notable feature is the stark gender inequity in the workforce structure in Bihar. While the share of females in the category of 'cultivators' is less than that of males, their share in the category of 'agriculture labourer' is substantially higher (Figure 2.7).

The lack of productive opportunities for females has resulted in a highly suboptimal work participation rates for females in rural Bihar. The NSSO report 531 on 'Employment and Unemployment Situation in India (July 2007-June 2008) shows that the work participation rate (WPR) for females in Bihar stood substantially below other states (NSSO, 2010b).

The report of the Equity Foundation (2011) brings out the human emotions behind such low participation rates. It notes, 'Our husbands migrate to other states and we are left alone, we feel very insecure. All of us have to work but since our village is very remote and prone to flood we have to go to faraway villages to work leaving our little children and old members behind us.'

Figure 2.7

Bihar: Employment by Sector

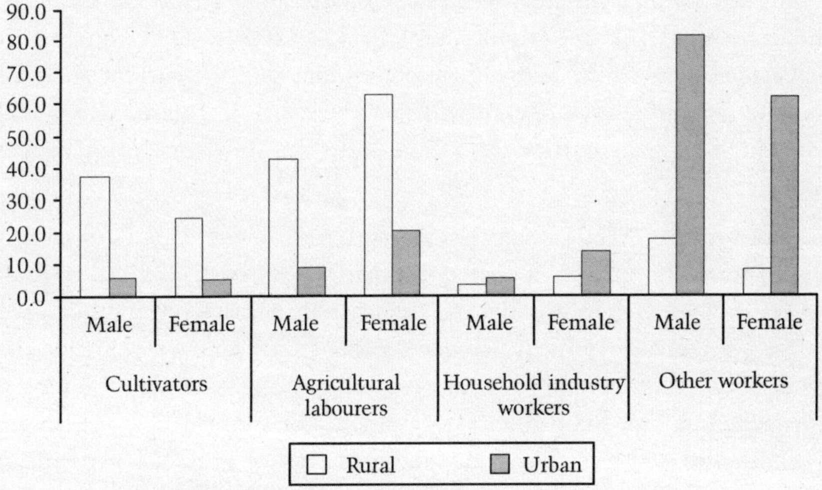

Source: *Bihar Economic Survey 2010-11*, Government of Bihar.

Table 2.13

WPR (per 1,000) according to Usual Status (PS+SS) by MPCE Quintile Classes (State-wise)

States	*MPCE Quintile Classes*					
	0-20	*20-40*	*40-60*	*60-80*	*80-100*	*All Classes*
Andhra Pradesh	476	462	519	483	412	471
Bihar	126	151	158	161	152	149
Gujarat	310	353	369	402	368	359
Haryana	218	279	289	292	317	278
Karnataka	364	401	422	396	378	392
Kerala	185	220	206	236	260	221
Madhya Pradesh	323	346	317	336	276	320
Maharashtra	397	442	475	463	405	436
Orissa	300	341	300	286	237	293
Punjab	184	223	238	246	304	238
Rajasthan	306	354	377	416	402	370
Tamil Nadu	343	402	419	437	342	389
Uttar Pradesh	191	186	190	192	193	190
West Bengal	167	151	154	144	114	146

Note: MPCE - Monthly Per Capita Expenditure.
Source: NSSO (2010b).

The Navodaya Shahar model has a special significance for this workforce scenario.

The study by Ekta Parishad and Praxis, referred to above states, 'in the entire area covered under the study, only 1.85 per cent of all land owners are women, owning a mere 1.84 per cent of the total area occupied by all land holdings' (Ekta Parishad and Praxis, 2009). Distribution of homegarden plots in the name of women in line with the current policy of the state government is likely to correct the above imbalance. This will have much larger significance as the following evidence from Kerala suggest.

In a study of Kerala, wage earning families who cultivate homegarden plots occupying a fraction of an acre, Kumar (1978) found that the value of homegarden production was the most consistent positive predictor of child nutrition in households in which the mother is not employed outside the home. This study concludes that given the strong correlation between homegardening and the presence of mothers not engaged in wage labour, distribution of land to landless and land-poor families may be a particularly fruitful strategy where employment opportunities for women are limited for societal or economic reasons.

Similarly, the rate of migration in the female population is substantially lower. Further, amongst the group that migrates, the 2001 Census showed that three-fourths are involved in intra-district migration. Thus, the Navodaya Shahar model which involves intra-district or perhaps intra-*taluka* mobility will be of significant importance to the low female work participation rate that is evident in Bihar.

2.7 Need for a 'Land Reform Plus' Approach to Uplift the Triple Bottom Line of the *Aam Admi*

The above discussion on the triple bottom line of the *aam admi* in rural Bihar brings home the realisation that deprivation is far more diverse and deep than the picture presented by the traditional measures of poverty or HDI. By concentrating resources and efforts in some areas, the state government has been able to record impressive results. But diversifying such results across all districts and to other sectors will not be possible unless the main structural issues are addressed.

The recommendation of LRC to provide asset to the assetless is of fundamental importance for this structural change. However, the fate of these recommendations points to the insights of some global experts, 'land reform to broaden rural land access is still desperately needed in India...the problems, however, will not be solved by relying solely on traditional land reform tools aiming to provide multiple acres for each land-poor household. Such goals are ideal, but often not feasible in the current political and fiscal environment. The central and state governments need to expand the number and type of tools in the land reform toolkit and prioritise improving land access for the most needy—those who have no land...Providing landless households with homestead plots fulfills the government's land reform and rural housing objectives' (Neilson *et al.*, 2006).

The approach suggested above has merit, but the canvass needs to be cast much broader given the spectre of deep multidimensional poverty in Bihar. Any scheme for allocating land to large number of households needs to be leveraged to give shape to habitat structures that could spur a host of complimentary services and livelihood opportunities. Only then will small plots of land succeed in creating viable livelihood platforms.

Human development services where the unmet needs are most profound, naturally emerge as a key complimentary area and an important source of future livelihood opportunities.

Further, distribution of small plots of land as a one-time exercise will not suffice. There is a need to create a dynamic livelihood platform that sets into motion a process of mobility and workforce transition. This is also necessary for reorganising farming land to achieve best results.

As noted above, supplementing traditional land reform instruments with market-based mechanisms for securing land to small and marginal farmers and the landless as suggested by the Steering Group on Agriculture is the right direction to go. But again, while land as an agricultural asset is important for providing the foundation for livelihood, there is a need to go much beyond seeing land in a pure individual agricultural asset perspective. This particularly holds in a scenario where the units are small and the numbers involved are large. It is important to integrate this asset creation aspect with other initiatives such as credit infrastructure, storage, processing and value addition, marketing etc. It is important to go even further into human development services on the one hand, and a whole range of community services and enterprises on the other. Such integration could transform a programme for distribution of small units of land to individual households into a dynamic inclusive growth momentum. This is the crux of the 'land reform plus' agenda.

Normally this agenda is carried on the wings of rural-urban transformation. But the demographic structure in Bihar has already reached a configuration that renders it incapable of dealing with the huge backlog. Thus, this transformation will have to be carried forward through a carefully designed programme of 'land reform plus'.

But how will such a complex task be achieved? The answer is that what looks to be quite a complex process is actually organic in nature. Once structural road blocks are removed, the process will gather momentum on its own. The Navodaya Shahar model embodying the 'land reform plus' approach seeks to create a secure highway in so far as the poor households are concerned. Security would come from asset ownership, access to services, and the fact that the mobility is designed not to abruptly change either the occupational pattern or the social moorings of households.

But if on the contrary, the 'land reform plus' agenda is couched as a pure public administration effort at land redistribution or for poverty alleviation, it is bound to fail at the very start. Thus, the fate that the LRC recommendation met is neither incidental nor surprising. LRC put forth its recommendation as a pure land redistribution agenda and the political leadership baulked.

Each of the following chapters attempts to draw out relevant aspects of this 'land reform plus' approach. However, such layering may at times seem repetitive!

Chapter 6 shows how the recommendations of LRC can be moved forward by combing it with the 'land reform plus' approach embedded in the Navodaya Shahar model. It also shows how the basic model can be advanced by combining it with the market-based approach suggested by the Steering Group on Agriculture (GoB, 2010).

3 Fragile Base of the New Resurgent Bihar

3.1 Resurgence Post-2005

The previous chapter explored Bihar's rural baseline in terms of the 'triple bottom line' of the *aam admi*. This chapter takes a look at the state's recent macroeconomic trends as well as some key sectoral trends impacting rural livelihood.

Overall, a picture of sharp resurgence based on the release of pent-up consumer demand emerges. This was duly reinforced by a revival in governmental spending across various sectors. During 2004-05 to 2010-11, Bihar's economy expanded at an annual rate of 10.93 per cent at constant prices. This was nearly three times the growth rate of 3.50 per cent over 1999-2000. In terms of current prices, the growth rate during 2004-05 to 2010-11 was 16.86 per cent per annum. Bihar surpassed almost all other states in term of its growth performance.

This resurgence was led by the construction sector where growth rates above 30 per cent per annum were recorded. In telecommunications, Bihar registered around 10-fold increase between 2005-06 and 2010-11 as the total number of connections increased from 4.2 million to 41.5 million. This explosion was mainly due to mobile connections which expanded by more than 17 times.

Between 2005-06 and 2009-10, the total number of registered vehicles recorded a four-fold increase from 0.08 million to 3.2 million. The annual increase in 2006-07 over 2005-06 was 83 per cent!

But again, there are clear signs of growing structural friction. Large inter-district disparity in efforts, performance and attainment is an important facet of such structural rigidities. The Patna district with a per capita GSDP of Rs 37,737 (estimates for 2006-07 at 1999-2000 constant prices) stands out. The next come far behind. These are Munger (Rs 12,370) and Begusarai (Rs 10,409). At the other end of the scale, the three most economically underdeveloped districts are Jamui (Rs 5,516), Araria (Rs 5,245) and Sheohar (Rs 4,398). The per capita GSDP of the latter set of districts is nearly six times lower than the all-India average.

Table 3.1

Yearly Growth Rate of GSDP (2005-06 to 2010-11 at 2004-05 Prices)

Sector	*2005-06*	*2006-07*	*2007-08*	*2008-09 (P)*	*2009-10 (Q)*	*2010-11 (Projected)*
1. Agriculture/an. hus.	-7.32	31.06	-6.81	11.32	-7.32	-7.32
2. Forestry/logging	-2.04	-2.21	-1.99	-2.03	-2.02	-2.06
3. Fishing	4.49	-6.62	7.47	7.17	-1.08	2.14
4. Mining/quarrying	61.04	-8.86	-1.41	-0.08	-0.12	7.64
Sub-total primary	**-6.02**	**24.93**	**-5.78**	**9.80**	**-6.56**	**-6.36**
5. Manufacturing	-9.04	5.16	25.16	-1.84	-0.05	3.44
5.1 Registered	-44.57	-17.01	123.86	-8.36	-0.11	-1.17
5.2 Un-registered	3.21	9.26	11.28	0.00	-0.03	4.64
6. Construction	36.91	34.78	25.00	8.48	32.09	27.01
7. Elec./wat. sup/gas	3.69	4.97	7.60	9.12	7.19	6.49
Sub-total secondary	**12.25**	**20.69**	**23.40**	**5.20**	**20.26**	**19.54**
8. Trans. storage/comm.	9.52	12.96	9.23	9.35	8.50	10.67
8.1 Railways	10.94	14.7	9.48	8.55	8.55	10.42
8.2 Other transport	2.41	8.08	4.25	4.94	1.90	4.29
8.3 Storage	-2.89	12.65	9.65	6.30	6.25	6.26
8.4 Communication	21.11	18.28	15.83	15.87	16.00	17.40
9. Trade/hotel/restaurant	-2.20	28.19	21.01	21.54	23.04	17.80
Sub-total (8&9)	**0.38**	**24.53**	**18.44**	**19.09**	**20.36**	**16.62**
10. Banking/insurance	13.77	19.93	11.59	20.37	16.35	16.35
11. REODB	9.05	9.53	9.44	9.78	10.12	9.58
Sub-total (10 & 11)	**10.89**	**13.68**	**10.35**	**14.29**	**12.92**	**12.71**
12. Public administration	-1.26	0.37	3.46	8.54	21.98	6.30
13. Other services	7.24	2.28	3.21	7.66	10.59	6.15
Sub-total tertiary	**3.37**	**14.64**	**12.36**	**15.11**	**17.54**	**13.28**
Total GSDP	**1.57**	**18.48**	**8.42**	**12.07**	**11.7**	**10.05**

Note: REODB - Real Estate, Ownership of Dwelling, Legal and Business Services.

Source: *Bihar Economic Survey 2010-11*, Government of Bihar.

Thus, the story of development in Bihar needs to move to the next level—from proximate quantitative gains to structural transformation. This is going to be a far more complex task. But aligned to the needs and energy of the *aam admi*, the returns are likely to be far more spectacular and sustained.

3.2 Agriculture

Agriculture is the backbone of Bihar's economy. Highly fertile soil in the riverine plane of the Ganga Basin, abundant surface water and ground water resources, a variety of agro-climatic conditions across its region (some which are highly conducive to production of fruits and other high value added products such as floriculture) and availability of abundant human resources are seen as major areas of comparative advantage.

The agricultural economy in Bihar is predominantly oriented towards subsistence production. As much as 95 per cent of the cropped area is under food grains. The oilseeds, fibres and sugarcane together account for barely 5 per cent of the cropped area. Rice, wheat and maize are the major crops. However, barring maize and pulses, productivity of farm produce in Bihar is much below the national average. The average yields of rice, wheat and maize are only about 30 to 40 per cent of the potential yield

Agriculture in Bihar is subject to a variety of risks arising from rainfall aberrations and natural calamities, especially floods. As is evident from Table 3.1, an increase in the real NSDP of agriculture in a year is regularly followed by a decline in NSDP the following year, and the magnitude of fluctuation is quite high. Weak rural infrastructure, imperfect markets, and the lack of financial services as well as suitable risk mitigation instruments exacerbate these risks.

Small and marginal farmers comprising 93 per cent of the state's agricultural community suffer from a number of handicaps. An overwhelmingly large share of the leased-in land is unrecorded and unregulated. Further, as indicated earlier, the average size of holdings is 0.60 hectare, and that too is divided on an average into 3.3 parcels. As a result, small and marginal farmers are not able to access the benefits of various facilities such as subsidised inputs, credit or extension services.

The agricultural markets suffer from some structural weaknesses. According to the Report of the Steering Group on Vision of Agriculture Development in Bihar (GoB, 2010), 'more than 90 per cent of the farmers sell their produce in villages, mainly to itinerant traders, at much lower prices than the procurement price of the respective agricultural commodities. There are very few procurement centers and a majority of them do not operate regularly. In view of the scale and objectives of agricultural growth envisaged in the coming years, the problems afflicting the systems and structures of agricultural marketing have to be addressed on a priority basis.' The Steering Group recommends the use of NABARD's Rural Infrastructure Development Fund for this purpose. It notes, 'investment in this area is basically a commercial activity. The government can create an enabling environment for private entrepreneurs.'

At the same time, the Steering Group points to some major structural changes that are taking shape in the agriculture sector of the state in recent years. The share of the crop sub-sector in the total value of agricultural output declined from around 66 per cent in TE 2001 to about 48 per cent in TE 2006. On the other hand, there was a steep increase in the share of the livestock from about 26 per cent in TE 2001 to 41 per cent in TE 2006. Some increase was also observed in the fishery sector. The importance of fruits and vegetables is increasing in Bihar's agricultural economy. The share of milk among the livestock products too is increasing.

The Report of the Steering Group concludes, 'over a period of time, there has been some diversification in the state's agriculture. However due to low productivity, which has shown a further decline since 2000, and low value realisation, this has not led to any measurable increase in income. The average per worker income in agriculture in Bihar is half of the average income of the agricultural worker in India. The main challenge, therefore, is to reverse the declining trend in productivity and to boost the growth momentum in some of the sub-sectors, primarily dairying.' (GoB, 2010)

The Steering Group on Agriculture has made a range of recommendations towards increasing productivity in agriculture so as to reach the average attained by the country in the next five years and equalling the best among the states of the country during the subsequent five years. Apart from identifying a host of institutional, technical and infrastructure development issues, these recommendations include creation of market-based mechanisms for augmenting land supply for the small and marginal farmers at fair prices. As indicated earlier, the Steering Group's emphasis on market-based mechanisms for securing land to small and medium farmers is equally relevant for implementing the government's land reforms objective with regard to the landless. This approach fits in well with the 'land reform plus' agenda outlined in the previous chapter.

Agriculture has emerged as the topmost priority of the NDA government in its second term starting November 2010. In April 2011, the Chief Minister, Nitish Kumar set up the first of a kind 'special cabinet on agriculture' to draw up a model for agriculture in the state. The 'special cabinet' has set up 14 committees: on water, cooperative, agriculture, animal husbandry, fisheries, disaster management, soil conservation, research, biotech, information technology, and market storage and processing.

While formulating a strategy based on the outputs of the above committees, however, it is important to keep in mind that given the population size dependant on agriculture, developing this lead sector in Bihar to its full potential is not a sectoral agenda and certainly not a narrow technical challenge. The reform canvass in the context of Bihar will have to be far broader than the input oriented strategy deployed during the first green revolution. As stressed earlier, an all encompassing re-organisation of the rural economy and society will have to be initiated and nurtured.

The turnaround in agriculture in Gujarat during the last decade has some relevant lessons although the context there was different in some respects. Shah *et al.* (2009) stress, 'in interpreting these regional trends, we have taken the view that public policies and investments and private enterprise and initiative have come together to create Gujarat's agricultural miracle. Excellent road networks, government initiatives to reform agricultural marketing institutions, a reinvented agricultural research and extension system, and improved infrastructure have laid the ground for rapid growth. The role of the private sector in ushering in the Bt cotton revolution cannot be overstated.'

Perhaps, given the context of Gujarat, Shah *et al.* (2009) has taken the role of rural-urban network for granted. It is inconceivable that the desired service network will materialise in the populous districts of Siwan (population size 3.3 million in 2011), Samastipur (4.25 million) and Madhubani (4.47 million) with just one Class II town and two or three

Class III or IV towns. A network of intermediate habitats will have to be established. This will be particularly important for attracting the private sector into direct commercial activities and in evolving PPP.

One area where private sector partnership will be crucial is agri-extension. The Steering Group on Agriculture concludes, 'as in several other parts of the country, the weakest link in agriculture in Bihar too is extension. This is evident from the fact that a dismal 0.4 per cent of farmers in Bihar received information on modern technology from extension agents. This is the lowest percentage among the major Indian states. The main sources of information on technology are the input suppliers and progressive farmers. There are three main public players for agricultural technology dissemination in Bihar. These institutions are Krishi Vigyan Kendras (KVKs), government departments and the Agricultural Technology Management Agency (ATMA)... The extension system, which was largely dysfunctional, may get a lease of life with the introduction of the Agricultural Technology Management Agency (ATMA), with its emphasis on decentralised decision-making, and integration of all related departments. However, the studies conducted by the World Bank and other agencies have also pointed out certain weaknesses in the performance of this model in the state' (GoB, 2010).

It is surprising that after noting such serious weaknesses, the Steering Group goes on to make the usual set of recommendations such as filing up vacancies, adequate autonomy, training and capacity building, better coordination, regular monitoring etc. There is a need to create a new PPP-based agri-extension framework to derive the maximum out of the vast assets that the present defunct system sits on and the large financial resources it consumes on a recurring basis (Box 3.1).

The Navodaya Shahar model outlined in Chapter 6 seeks to establish intermediate level habitats that could host the maize of services recommended by the Steering Group on Agriculture, and create suitable conditions for modern private companies to set base close to the point of action. That the direct benefits of such habitats in terms of agriculture production can be quite substantial in itself is clear from the evidence with regard to small home and garden plots presented in Chapter 6.

Box 3.1

Creating a Vibrant Public-Private-Panchayat Partnership for Inclusive Growth through Inclusive Governance: Need for a New PPPP-based Agri-Extension Framework

This study concludes that at the core of the weak rural economy is the weak and unresponsive public extension framework in agriculture and allied sectors. While this has been highlighted in numerous studies as well as in public documents including the working group reports of the Planning Commission, the remedial measures suggested have been partial or incremental in nature, especially in so far as delegation of power to local governance institutions and partnership with the private sector are concerned.

The *panchayat* level leaders also do not see any direct role for themselves in agriculture and place this responsibility (infact, the opportunity!) at the door of other agencies such as cooperatives and government departments. This report concludes that in order to gain their true place in the rural economy, PRIs must transform this narrow and lopsided vision of their own mandate and accept a direct leadership role in agriculture which is the mainstay of the rural economy. The PPPP-based rural service enterprise model suggested in the report may be a good opportunity in this regard. A direct leadership role of PRIs in agriculture would provide the foundation for convergence of other developmental activities in rural areas. A mainframe monitoring role and responsibility for PRIs under the proposed model will also serve to equip them with the much needed resource support.

A number of business agencies have built up impressive capacities and networks in input supply and extension services. This has generated intense public debate on the merits and demerits of the role of the business sector in agriculture and on institutional arrangements such as contact farming, contract farming and corporate farming. A Planning Commission report concludes, 'private traders enjoy oligopolies in supply of seeds and other inputs on credit...this results in exploitation of poor farmers on the one hand, and their poor information base on the other hand.' Some point to the risks of moving away from subsistence-based farming system and into the vagaries of the market-risks. At the same time, there is a constituency that points to the benefits being derived by farmers who were unable to tap new opportunities on their own. Also, there is growing evidence that as a part of their strategy for transacting with large numbers of small farmers, business firms are

contd...

...contd...

taking steps that have an empowering effect on the former (e.g., formation of producer companies). Thus casting this divide in stone will not be a prudent approach.

This study outlines a PPPP-based rural service enterprise model that could leverage the assets and resources currently deployed through pubic agri-extension system to create an orgainsed, accountable and responsive extension mechanism guaranteeing a menu of services.

Towards a workable PPPP-based mechanism, the study advocates for a shift from a CSR–type approach to a more formal legal and institutional framework-based approach, and for measures to reduce transaction costs which are enormously high not only because of weak physical infrastructure, but also on account of restrictive rules combined with large grey areas where taking any partnership initiative requires long, cumbersome and costly efforts at breaking new grounds. It calls for public policy support to PPPP to move away from incremental or partial measures such as allocation of some resources for subsiding PPPP initiatives to addressing the core issues and institutional bottlenecks responsible for the enormously high transaction costs in such initiatives.

The study highlights that most vital link in the PPPP chain is the strengthening of community capacity. This includes issues such as property rights for the poor, both for the assets held individually and for community resources. Without clear property rights, local actors will not be able to partner with the organised sector, nor can they muster resources such as credit to join new ventures.

Source: Singh (2010a).

The dynamic perspective of the Navodaya Shahar model is also of importance to agriculture. By providing a bridge for safe transition from farming into a more hybrid livelihood base that includes new opportunities symbiotic to a prospering agricultural base, the Navodaya Shahar model is likely to help arrest the trend towards ceaseless fragmentation of all land masses in the countryside into unviable units.

3.3 State of the Rural Enterprises

According to the ASI report, Bihar with 8 per cent of India's population had a share of mere 1.22 per cent in the factories in India (2007-08). The percentage of factories in operation in the state was lower than the all-India average. The agro-based industries accounted for 88 per cent of the total value added of Rs 1,159 crore from all industrial units. If the remaining small and micro units are included, the share of agro-based industries will be even larger. Food products/beverages/tobacco group contributed over 76 per cent of the total net value added by all the factories in operation in Bihar.

According to the Fourth Census of the MSME sector (2006-07), about 21 per cent of the units were closed and around 6 per cent were non-traceable. Of the closed units, 40.6 per cent units were in rural areas.

The data on the operation of the District Industries Centres (DICs) provides some important conclusions. Even if one ignores the trend in percentage achievement *vis-à-vis* the targets as the latter may be over-ambitious, the decline in the absolute numbers since 2007-08 except in distribution of credit cards to small entrepreneurs, stands out.

The sharp decline under the Prime Minister's Employment Generation Programme (PMEGP) or the former Rural Employment Generation Programme (REGP) after 2007-08 shows that the absorptive capacity for enterprises in rural areas is quite limited.

The district-wise report on PMEGP for 2010-11 (upto October 2010) provided in the *Bihar Economic Survey 2010-11* shows that this programme is generating very little enterprise activity and employment in absolute terms. The result is totally insignificant when compared to the population of the districts and their needs. This is the picture with regard to many other programmes. Such solutions have no relevance. They need to be scrapped in favour of few large initiatives aimed at direct transfer of assets and activities such as creation of rural markets.

Table 3.2

Achievement of DIC under Different Programmes

Year	Target	Achievement: Number	Achievement: Loan Amount/ Investment (Rs lakh)	Achievement as Percentage of Targets
Establishment of small industries				
2006-07	7000	7104	7279.79	101.48
2007-08	7000	7202	13482.98	102.90
2008-09	8000	6154	11886.06	76.93
2009-10	8000	5091	12864.46	63.64
2010-11 (upto Sept. 2010)	8000	1552	8381.75	19.40
Artisan credit cards				
2006-07	6250	8708	3262.09	139.33
2007-08	23491	10607	15820.53	45.00
2008-09	25000	7055	2398.57	28.22
2009-10	25000	3071	1015.66	12.28
2010-11 (upto Sept 2010)	25000	274	351.70	1.10
Small entrepreneur's credit card				
2006-07	2500	3200	4334.64	128.00
2007-08	15000	5140	11487.23	34.00
2008-09	15000	6265	19422.83	41.77
2009-10	15000	7008	49716.44	46.72
2010-11 (upto Sept 2010)	15000	356	114109.81	2.37
Rural Employment Generation Programme (REGP/PMEGP)				
2006-07	638	1066	2178.27	167.08
2007-08	718	1184	3020.61	165.00
2008-09	2147	236	299.27	10.99
2009-10	2147	564	891.94	26.27
2010-11 (upto Sept. 2010)	2503	268	349.80	10.71

Source: *Bihar Economic Survey 2010-11*, Government of Bihar.

Table 3.3

Progress in PMEGP 2010-11 (upto October 2010)

			Application Sanctioned			
District	Population 2011	Proportion of Rural Population in 2001 (%)	No.	Project Amount (Rs in lakh)	Margin Money Involved (Rs in lakh)	Employment (No.)
Araria	28.06	93.9	3	9.97	2.99	17
Arwal	6.99	NA	1	2.7	0.67	3
Aurangabad	25.11	91.6	19	67.2	20.83	58
Banka	20.29	96.5	0	0	0	0
Begusarai	29.54	95.4	58	60.36	19.43	103
Bhagalpur	30.32	81.3	41	224.78	64.69	206
Bhojpur	27.2	86.1	8	33.75	8.55	31
Buxar	17.07	90.8	25	162.23	47.25	59
Darbhanga	39.21	91.9	10	39.95	10.43	41
E.Champaran	50.82	93.6	1995	100	25.45	100
Gaya	43.79	86.3	0	0	0	0
Gopalganj	25.58	93.9	20	129	41.9	107
Jamui	17.56	92.6	3	13	4	17
Jehanabad	11.24	91.6	2	9.6	3	2
Kaimur	16.29	96.8	16	146.87	45	74
Katihar	30.68	90.9	2	4	1.4	4
Khagaria	16.57	94.0	7	79.37	24.85	80
Kishanganj	16.9	90.0	24	43.65	11.83	46
Lakhisarai	10.00	85.3	2	15	3.25	13
Madhepura	19.94	95.9	8	24.5	2.27	46
Madhubani	44.76	96.5	20	100	5	100
Munger	13.59	72.1	2	10	2.5	10
Muzaffarpur	47.78	90.7	3	17.12	5.94	22
Nalanda	29.72	85.1	24	78.92	19.52	91
Nawada	22.16	92.6	0	0	0	0
Patna	57.72	58.4	71	666.64	139.47	570
Purnea	32.73	91.3	5	59.4	19.79	56
Rohtas	29.62		36	405.48	101.11	262
Saharsa	18.97	91.7	0	0	0	0
Samastipur	42.54	96.4	60	337.57	113.93	307
Saran	39.43	90.8	3	20	7	17
Sheikhpura	6.34	84.5	0	0	0	0
Sheohar	6.56	95.6	5	11	2.9	8
Sitamarhi	34.19	94.3	4	23	3.55	25
Siwan	33.18	94.5	8	65	22.25	36
Supaul	22.28	94.9	1	8	2.8	0
Vaishali	34.94	93.1	5	36.45	12.75	46
W.Champaran	39.22	89.8	432	110	14.53	52
Total	1038.89	3250.7	519	3114.51	810.83	2609

Source: *Bihar Economic Survey 2010-11*, Government of Bihar.

The *Bihar Economic Survey 2010-11* reports that the handloom sector in the state 'has seen a gradual decline over time and today the sector remains largely a story of impoverished weavers. Only around 10,850 handlooms are operating under 1,090 weavers' cooperative societies. Out of 38 districts in the state, the handloom units are concentrated in 14 districts, important among them being Patna, Gaya, Madhubani, Siwan, Bhagalpur and Nalanda. The study conducted by IL&FS reiterates that most of the weavers were still operating on a very small scale and do not have a commercially sustainable size of operation. There is a necessity to federate the weavers and bring their operations to a viable scale.'

Small enterprises and home-based work in rural areas have 'potential' advantages in terms of certain cost elements and availability of certain raw materials. For example, according to a recent survey conducted by the Association for Social and Economic Transformation (ASET), around 33 per cent of total horticulture produce in Bihar goes waste. The losses of mango and tomato have been as high as 39 per cent in major horticulture producing districts of the state. But where rural-urban linkages go extremely thin, as is the case with most districts in Bihar, these advantages are lost. The markets in Patna are better connected with the cotton mills in Kanpur than with the weavers in rural clusters in the Nalanda district.

As discussed in the previous chapter, lack of non-farm employment opportunities has meant that a large part of the marginal farmers has no option but to move into the ranks of landless labour upon fragmentation of land or other agriculture related shocks. Women have tended to move out of the workforce. These in turn have further impoverished the base of rural enterprises.

To conclude, the growth of rural enterprises and that of distributed industrialisation more generally is again not a sectoral agenda. The Navodaya Shahar model applies equally to this sector.

3.4 Banking Infrastructure, Deposits and Credit

The financial sector not only defines the current health of the economy but also determines its future growth prospects. Trends in the credit-deposit ratio (CD ratio) in Bihar and its comparison across states reveal a story of large structural barriers to growth.

The CD ratio in Bihar in 2001-02 was 22.79 per cent. Thus, this poor state was utilising barely a fifth of the financial resources that it was generating. The CD ratio improved to 33.81 per cent in 2006-07. But it seems to have hit severe resistance at around this level.

Table 3.4

CD Ratio of All Banks in Bihar

Year	*Deposit (Rs crore)*	*Credit (Rs crore)*	*CD Ratio*
2001-02	30,482	6,946	22.79
2002-03	33,815	8,089	23.92
2003-04	35,824	9,604	26.81
2004-05	40,295	12,031	29.86
2005-06	46,134	14,808	32.10
2006-07	56,342	19,048	33.81
2007-08	68,244	22,077	32.35
2008-09	83,048	24,051	28.96
2009-10	98,588	31,679	32.13
2010-11 (till June 2010)	99,636	32,109	32.23

Source: *Bihar Economic Survey 2010-11*, Government of Bihar.

The CD ratio in Bihar is less than half the national average. It is also much lower than in comparable states such as Rajasthan, Orissa and Uttar Pradesh (see Figure 3.1). Reaching the national average will generate investible resources of over Rs 30,000 crore. Success in attaining the CD ratio of Andhra Pradesh would translate into additional investible resources of Rs 65,000 to 70,000 crore.

A disaggregation of the CD ratio shows that the Scheduled Commercial Banks (SCBs) which mobilise the bulk of the deposits in the state are the biggest laggards in so far as advances and investments in the state are concerned.

Figure 3.1

CD Ratio of Major Indian States as of March 2010 (%)

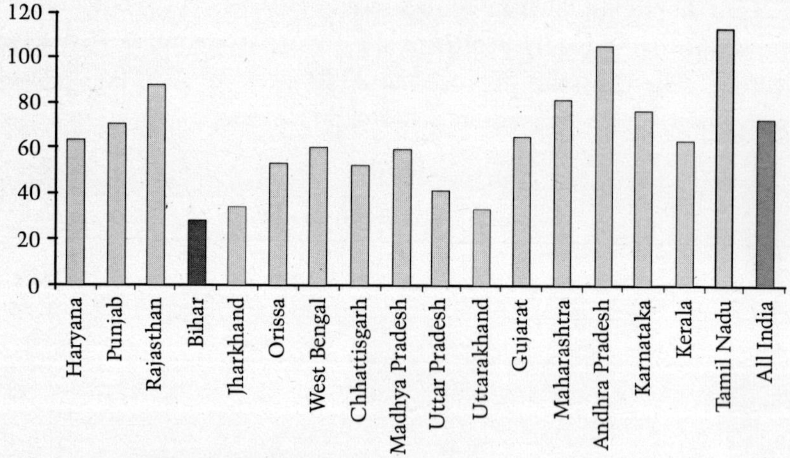

Source: *Bihar Economic Survey 2010-11*, Government of Bihar.

Table 3.5

Bank Group-wise and Area-wise CD Ratio in Bihar (31.06.2010)

Bank Group	*Area*	*Deposit (Rs crore)*	*Advances/ Investment (Rs crore)*	*CD Ratio (%)*
Commercial banks	Rural	17385	6317	36.33
	Semi-urban	22858	6611	28.92
	Urban-metro	45557	11898	26.12
	Total	85800	24826	28.93
RRBs	Rural	8701	3671	42.19
	Semi-urban	2390	738	30.86
	Urban-metro	1221	352	28.85
	Total	12312	4760	38.66
Cooperative banks	Rural	NA	NA	NA
	Semi-urban	NA	NA	NA
	Urban-metro	1525	632	41.42
	Total	1525	632	41.42
All banks	Rural	26086	9987	38.29
	Semi-urban	25248	7348	29.1
	Urban-metro	48302	12882	26.67
	Total	99636	30217	30.33

Source: *Bihar Economic Survey 2010-11*, Government of Bihar.

An interstate comparison of the CD ratio of SCBs across states exacerbates the picture of their skewed operations in Bihar.

Figure 3.2

Per Capita Deposits and Credits of SCBs as on 31st March 2010 (Rs)

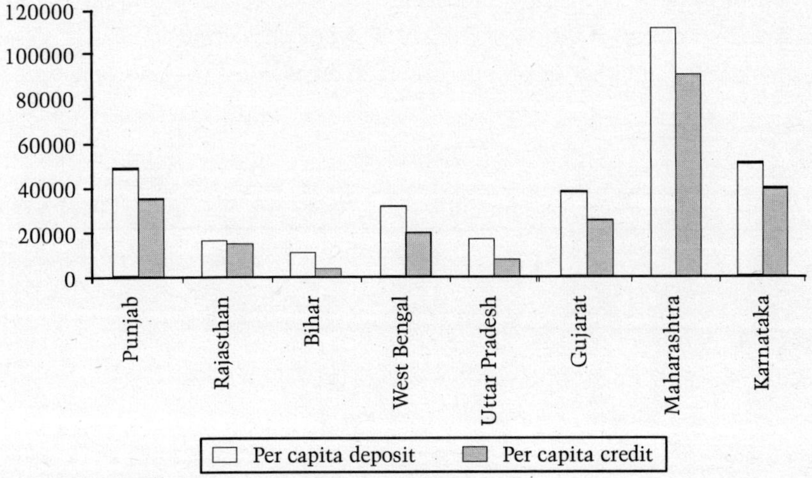

Source: *Bihar Economic Survey 2010-11*, Government of Bihar.

The *Bihar Economic Survey 2010-11* attributes the state's abysmal CD ratio to the paucity of bank branches in the state. It states that Bihar has 8 per cent of the country's population, but 'with a share of less than 5 per cent of the total number of bank branches in India, 3 per cent of total employees of scheduled commercial banks, and with only 2 per cent share of total deposits and less than 1 per cent share of the total bank credits in the country, Bihar still remains one of the most disadvantaged states in the country in terms of banking.'

A comparison of the CD ratio across urban and rural areas presented in Table 3.5 shows that these ratios are higher in rural areas than in semi-urban or urban-metro areas. This is, however, a misleading picture resulting from much lower deposits from rural areas in SCBs and the need for these banks to maintain a certain minimum priority sector lending in view of the RBI regulations. An interesting finding is the relatively higher levels of both deposits and credits in semi-urban areas relative to its size in the economy and demography of Bihar.

Table 3.6 shows that nearly 60 per cent of bank branches in Bihar are in rural areas. Thus, despite the context of relatively high rural-urban ratio in Bihar, in this parameter, the state seems to compare well with other states. But again there is a need to look at not just the number of banks but their nature and business mobilisation. Also, the recent trend presented in Table 3.7 shows a movement towards a declining rural share. The *Bihar Economic Survey 2010-11* indicates that during 2009-10, of the 214 new branches opened in Bihar, all but 44 were opened in either urban or semi-urban areas. Most of these were opened by private non-nationalised banks.

Table 3.6

Distribution of Branches of Commercial Banks among States (2008-09)

State	*% Share in State Total*			*State Total*	*% Share in All-India*
	Rural	*Semi-Urban*	*Urban*		
Andhra Pradesh	35.52	22.87	41.61	6746	8.15
Bihar	59.72	21.66	18.62	3942	4.76
Gujarat	33.04	22.04	44.92	4492	5.43
Haryana	31.26	21.64	47.11	2214	2.67
Karnataka	35.19	20.00	44.81	6010	7.26
Kerala	7.84	64.90	27.26	4211	5.09
Madhya Pradesh	42.90	23.85	33.25	4096	4.95
Maharashtra	26.87	18.13	55.01	7961	9.62
Orissa	60.07	18.60	21.33	2752	3.32
Punjab	33.52	28.8	37.67	3371	4.07
Rajasthan	43.33	24.64	32.02	4050	4.89
Tamil Nadu	27.75	30.22	42.04	6159	7.44
Uttar Pradesh	48.54	18.04	33.41	9921	11.98
West Bengal	44.5	12.03	43.47	5211	6.29
All India	31676	19213	31905	82794	100

Source: *Bihar Economic Survey 2010-11*, Government of Bihar.

Table 3.7

Distribution of Commercial Bank Branch Offices in Bihar

Year (End-March)	*Total*	*Growth Rate (%)*	*% Share in Total*		
			Rural	*Semi-Urban*	*Urban*
2005	3648	0.69	64.80	20.07	15.13
2006	3675	0.74	63.59	20.6	15.81
2007	3712	1.01	62.80	20.66	16.54
2008	3792	2.16	61.63	20.97	17.41
2009	3942	3.96	59.72	21.66	18.62
2010	4156	5.43	57.72	22.45	19.83

Source: *Bihar Economic Survey 2010-11*, Government of Bihar.

The state and the district central cooperative banks were set up to play a special role in agricultural credit. But Bihar has been a laggard in this area. The Steering Committee on Agriculture has called for steps to revive the agriculture cooperative machinery.

Regional Rural Banks (RRBs) were set up under the RRB Act of 1976 to effectively channelise resources towards agricultural and rural credit. With equity holdings by the Central Government, the concerned state governments and the sponsor bank in the proportion of 50:15:35, the RRBs provide a multi-agency approach for agricultural and rural credit in India.

There is a relatively higher concentration of RRBs in Bihar. Thus at the end of 2009, the ratio of deposit of RRBs in Bihar to the total rural deposits of all SCBs in the state stood at 43 per cent as against the national average of about 28 per cent.

Table 3.8

Branches and Deposits of Regional Rural Banks (2007-2009)

States	*December 2007*			*December 2008*			*December 2009*		
	No. of Branches	*Total Deposits (Rs crore)*	*Total Credit (Rs crore)*	*No. of Branches*	*Total Deposits (Rs crore)*	*Total Credit (Rs crore)*	*No. of Branches*	*Total Deposits (Rs crore)*	*Total Credit (Rs crore)*
Bihar	1429	7245	3027	1439	8917	3661	1439	8917	3661
Madhya Pradesh	975	5237	2971	986	5988	3394	986	5988	3394
Maharashtra	547	2192	1362	497	2120	1368	497	2120	1368
Rajasthan	975	5000	3543	992	6016	4096	992	6016	4096
Uttar Pradesh	2735	16529	8571	2774	19831	9576	2774	19831	9576
West Bengal	848	5258	3027	850	6119	2482	850	6119	2482
India	13846	76389	49381	14091	91289	55739	14091	91289	55739

Source: Bihar Economic Survey 2010-11, Government of Bihar.

Table 3.8 above presents a comparison of the growth rates in the deposits and credits of RRBs in Bihar with other states over December 2007 to December 2009. Given the higher overall growth rates in Bihar during this period, one would have expected a marked difference in the growth rates of deposits and credits *vis-à-vis* other states. But this is not visible. Is this again a warning signal in so far as the base for future rural growth trajectory in Bihar is concerned?

The utilisation pattern under RIDF brings out clearly the structural and institutional rigidities.

Table 3.9

Cumulative Disbursements under RIDF till March 2010

States	*Sanctions*	*Disbursements*	*Disbursement (%)*
Andhra Pradesh	11750	8090	69
Karnataka	5555	3491	63
Kerala	2951	1911	65
Tamil Nadu	7194	5585	78
Gujarat	8210	6281	77
Maharashtra	6634	4643	70
Haryana	2621	1816	69
Punjab	3925	2915	74
Rajasthan	6332	4197	66
Uttar Pradesh	8747	6223	71
Uttarakhand	1703	1076	63
Chhattisgarh	1569	1195	76
Madhya Pradesh	7532	4734	63
Bihar	3835	1815	47
Jharkhand	2480	1283	52
Orissa	4871	2617	54
West Bengal	6260	3826	61
All-India	103718	68440	66

Source: *Bihar Economic Survey 2010-11*, Government of Bihar.

RIDF was set up by the Government of India in 1995-96 for financing ongoing rural infrastructure projects. The fund is maintained by NABARD. Domestic commercial banks contribute to the fund to the extent of their shortfall in stipulated priority sector lending to agriculture. The main objective of the fund is to provide loans to state governments and state owned corporations to enable them to complete ongoing rural infrastructure projects. The scope of RIDF has been widened to include:

- Social sector investments such as rural health centres and primary schools, shishu shiksha kendras (SSKs) and *anganwadis*.
- Agriculture and allied sectors including irrigation projects, soil and water conservation, rain water harvesting etc. Activities include community irrigation wells, seed/agriculture/horticulture farms, plantation and horticulture, grading and certifying mechanisms such as testing and certifying laboratories, animal husbandry, riverine fisheries, watershed development/reclamation of waterlogged areas, flood protection, drainage, forest development etc.

- Rural infrastructure such as roads and bridges, mini-hydel plants, system improvement in the power sector, market yard/godown, *apna mandi, rural haats* and other marketing infrastructure, cold storage, modern abattoir, fishing harbour/jetties etc.

Till the end of 2009-10, 15 tranches (I to XV) of RIDF have been released covering total cumulative sanctions for Rs 1,03,718 crore for the entire country, out of which only Rs 68,440 crore (66%) have been disbursed.

The RIDF allocation to Bihar is much lower than what one would expect based on the criteria of population and gap in rural infrastructure. But even out of the small allocation, nearly 53 per cent remains unutilised till March 2010. The blame for this is likely to be put on understaffing in various concerned departments. But the malady is much deeper. Such a low utilisation rate points to a deficient vision regarding rural infrastructure.

The situation is not much better at the other end of the spectrum. The *Bihar Economic Survey 2010-11* states that achievements made under anti-poverty schemes like PMEGP and SGSY were annulled by the extremely low rate of recovery and concludes, 'overall, it appears that banking in Bihar is yet to start creating a real impact on the investment climate in the state.'

Similarly, the penetration of microfinance in Bihar is insignificant as compared to the other states in India. As on 31st March 2010 Bihar's share of all the SHGs in India was merely 1.69 per cent. The *Bihar Economic Survey*, ascribes this to, 'skewed distribution of SHGs across the districts, weak infrastructure that restricts outreach and effective support to groups, increasing costs and low efficiency, extremist activities, caste conflicts, lack of experience and capacity among the NGOs for microfinance, issues related to transition from grant-driven to revenue-based model, conservative attitude of bankers towards SHGs, fund constraints for start-ups, etc.'

The Bihar Rural Livelihood Project which is receiving World Bank (IDA) support to the tune of USD 63 million, aims to create 44,000 self-help groups (SHGs) covering 0.59 million households in 42 blocks in six districts of Bihar. In addition, the project is expected to receive USD 30 million from the Bank as part of the Kosi Flood Reconstruction and

Rehabilitation Project to expand its scale of operations to 13 more blocks across three districts. The target is to create 15,000 more SHGs covering 0.16 million households in these flood affected districts.

The above baseline in respect of the financial sector in Bihar reeks of underlying structural weaknesses. The CD ratios show sluggishness at a very suboptimal level. There are wide disparities across districts. The CD ratio is above 40 per cent in nine districts, but it is less than the 30 per cent in 17 of the state's 38 districts. The expansion of the banking infrastructure is showing a clear trend against rural areas. Overall, the trend displayed by the critical financial sector indicators does not bear out the story of the recent high growth rates. This does not augur well for sustaining the high rural growth rates in future.

On the other hand, the semi-urban areas seem to show vibrancy beyond the level warranted by its size. This shows that rural areas may be best served through suitable intermediate habitats. Private banks which are growing in strength and share across India, will be more inclined to set up base in smaller towns than in rural areas. The network of Navodaya Shahars proposed in this book would thus be critical for creating a platform for servicing the financial needs of the rural economy.

3.5 Development Expenditure: Trends and Priorities for Pro-Poor Development

Table 3.10 shows that in general, there has been a substantial increase in the per capita expenditure across different sub-sectors. The per capita capital outlay has increased steadily over the years from a meagre Rs 231 in 2005-06 and now stands at Rs 1,073.

Similarly, the per capita development expenditure (PCDE) in Bihar shows a sharp upward trend since 2005-06, and it even managed to narrow the gap with the national average between 2005-06 and 2007-08 (Figure 3.3). But since 2007-08, the gap has widened as the national average seems to be growing at a much faster pace. This gap is of significance. But the point of enquiry here is not the cause of such a gap as the state government seems to be doing its best in a fiscally responsible manner. The agenda is to explore how such meagre funds could be utilised to promote equity and create a multiplier effect.

Figure 3.3

Trend in per Capita Development Expenditure (2001-02 to 2010-11)

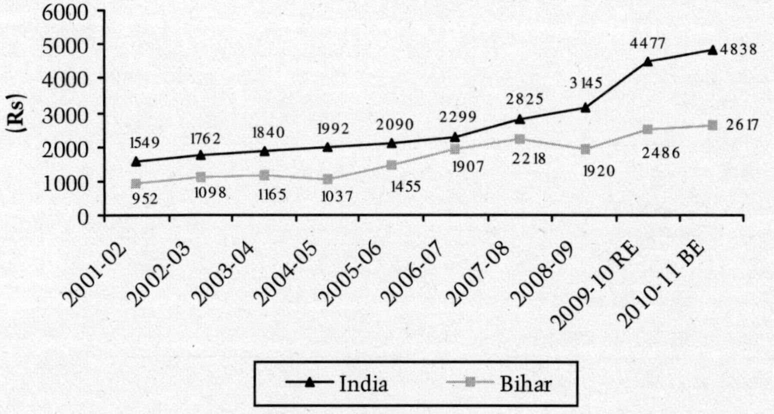

Source: *Bihar Economic Survey 2010-11*, Government of Bihar.

Table 3.10

Trend in Expenditure on Social and Economic Services

	2005-06	*2006-07*	*2007-08*	*2008-09*	*2009-10*	*2010-11 (BE)*
Estimated population (crore)	9.02	9.16	9.31	9.45	9.58	9.72
Total expenditure (Rs crore)						
Education, sports etc.	4394	5253	5496	6706	7416	9497
Medical and public health	877	985	1141	1193	1388	1911
Water supply and sanitation	407	514	713	1413	1438	2838
Social services	6862	7917	9868	12252	13186	17816
Economic services	2367	4021	4438	5726	7088	7410
Capital outlay	2084	5211	6104	6436	7332	10434
General services	8523	8643	9252	10530	12202	15448
Per capita expenditure (Rs)						
Education, sports etc.	487	573	590	710	774	977
Medical and public health	97	108	123	126	145	197
Water supply and sanitation	45	56	77	150	150	292
Social services	761	864	1060	1297	1376	1833
Economic services	262	439	477	606	740	762
Capital outlay	231	569	656	681	765	1073
General services	945	944	994	1114	1274	1589

Source: *Bihar Economic Survey 2010-11*, Government of Bihar.

Table 3.11

Extent of Disparity in Public Expenditure across Districts

Expenditure Heads	*Ratio of Maximum to Average (2008-09)*	*Ratio of Maximum to Average (2009-10)*	*Ratio of Minimum to Average (2008-09)*	*Ratio of Minimum to Average (2009-10)*
Primary education	9.1	6.7	0.2	0.4
Secondary education	3.2	3.9	0.2	0.4
Higher education	16.7	17.2	0.0	0.0
Medical	7.0	5.8	0.2	0.4
Drinking water supply	10.5	9.2	0.0	0.0
Welfare of SC, ST and OBC	3.8	8.1	0.3	0.2

Source: *Bihar Economic Survey 2010-11*, Government of Bihar.

A matter of great concern is the large intra-district disparity in allocation of public resources. In almost all social and economic sectors, the Patna district leads the table in allocation and consumption of public resources by a very wide margin. But this not only because of its population size. *Prima facie*, the use of public resources appears to be related to the size of the urban population of districts and particularly the population in Class I towns, rather than to the total district population and relative backwardness.

3.6 Conclusion

The above discussion brings home the fact that different sectors have their individual characteristics but they share a large common ground in terms of the people they employ and serve. Particularly, characteristics in terms of social organisation, property ownership, habitat structure, social services, connectivity etc., affect all sectors in any area, and the prospect of change in one area without a change in the overall baseline appears to be dim. This is particularly true when the baseline is trapped at a highly sub-optimal level. Thus, public efforts in major sectors such as agriculture, education and health need to promote such a baseline in a synergistic manner, and in return harness the benefits from the cross-sectoral energy.

In an environment of extreme stunting of rural-urban linkages, promotion of intermediate habitats that could serve as hubs for social and economic services becomes critical for promoting such synergy. This calls for a holistic vision for rural infrastructure. But the low utilisation rate in programmes such as RIDF points to the fact that the state government is yet to evolve such a holistic vision.

The rigid bifurcation of government functioning into 'rural development' and 'urban development' strands is one of the main contributors to this fragmentation in vision and efforts. The working of each on its own narrow agenda creates a roadblock in what is meant to be a natural and seamless process in the business of societies and the lives of the *aam admi*. This impedes the transformation process based on locally relevant solutions.

Now as the NDA government in Bihar sets out on a comprehensive programme for pro-poor development during its second term, it needs to confront these deeper structural factors. Major initiatives in areas such as land reforms, agriculture, education and health need to come together to create a network of habitats that contributes to achieving all these objectives in a synergistic manner.

In view of the modest resource base in relation to the development challenges, the state government needs to promote mechanisms to create a multiplier effect. Such efforts need to be made in all spheres. Given the experience over the last few years however, the chances of success appear to be brighter in the social sector and in small and medium entrepreneurial efforts.

This augurs well for pro-poor development. But it puts a responsibility on the state government to think of reforms in a fresh perspective. The government needs to create a policy regime cum legal framework that supports medium and small efforts, enterprises in social sectors, and initiatives in new areas such as habitat creation/upgradation in deep rural hinterland. This will require a new regime in PPP on the one hand, and a legal framework that protects the property rights of the poor and their belongings such as a *katcha* house on the other. This will be critical for generating safe and secure mobility for the poor in an otherwise highly risky environment (CLEP and UNDP, 2008).

This is the crux of the Navodaya Shahar model and the 'land reform plus approach' outlined in the previous chapter. Creation of assets for the *aam admi* in such habitats will be the point of departure for livelihood security, growth and democracy. This new reform agenda calls for a new organising principle—the Bihar Nav Nirman Programme.

4 Urbanisation Pattern and Implications for Rural Growth

4.1 Trends in Urbanisation in Bihar

This chapter explores the urbanisation pattern in Bihar. The relevant agenda however, is not urbanisation *per se*, but to attain a better understanding of the interplay between stunted urbanisation and rural stagnation, and its implications for human development and inclusive growth.

As per the 2011 Census, only 11.30 per cent of Bihar's total population is urban as against the national average of 31.16 per cent, and 48.45 per cent in Tamil Nadu, the most urbanised state in India. Between 2001 and 2011, the urban ratio in Bihar increased from 10.5 to 11.3 per cent while the all-India ratio increased from 27.81 per cent to 31.16 per cent.

In the decade 1971-1981, the rate of growth of urbanisation in Bihar was 4.3 per cent as compared to the national average of 3.1 per cent. However, by 1991-2001, it declined sharply to 2.6 per cent and stood below the national average of 2.7 per cent. Between 2001 and 2011, the decadal rate of urban growth in Bihar was 7.6 per cent as against the national average of 12.1 per cent.

The above gap is going to progressively widen. The 'Report of the Technical Group on Population Projections Constituted by the National Commission on Population' (May 2006) indicates that the urban ratio in Bihar will remain almost stagnant at the current low level upto 2026, the final year for which the projections have been made (GoI, 2006). Other major states will record a gain of between 7 to 30 per cent from their 2001 level.

Table 4.1

Trends in the Level and Rate of Urbanisation across Major States (1971-2001)

States	*Level of Urbanisation (in per cent)*					*Rate of Growth in Urbanisation (per annum)*			
	1971	*1981*	*1991*	*2001*	*2011*	*1971-81*	*1981-91*	*1991-2001*	*2001-2011*
Andhra Pradesh	19.31	23.32	26.89	27.08	33.49	2.08	1.53	0.07	2.36
Bihar	10.0	12.47	13.14	13.36	11.3	2.47	0.54	0.17	0.76
Gujarat	28.08	31.1	34.49	37.35	42.58	1.08	1.09	0.83	1.32
Haryana	17.66	21.88	24.63	29.00	34.79	2.39	1.26	1.77	1.99
Karnataka	24.31	28.89	30.92	33.98	38.57	1.88	0.7	0.99	1.34
Kerala	16.24	18.74	26.39	25.97	27.63	1.54	4.08	-0.16	0.63
Madhya Pradesh	31.17	20.3	23.21	24.92	47.72	2.45	1.43	0.74	1.25
Maharashtra	31.17	35.03	38.69	42.4	45.23	1.24	1.04	0.96	0.66
Orissa	8.41	11.79	13.38	14.97	16.68	4.02	1.35	1.19	1.12
Punjab	23.73	27.68	29.55	33.95	37.49	1.66	0.68	1.49	1.04
Rajasthan	17.63	21.05	22.88	23.38	24.89	1.94	0.87	0.22	0.64
Tamil Nadu	30.62	32.95	34.15	43.86	48.45	0.89	0.36	2.84	1.04
Uttar Pradesh	14.02	17.95	19.84	21.02	22.28	2.8	1.05	1.98	0.71
West Bengal	24.75	26.47	27.48	28.03	31.89	0.69	0.38	0.2	1.39
All-India	19.9	23.34	25.71	27.78	31.16	1.72	1.02	0.81	1.21

Source: GoI (2009) and Census (2011).

The Expert Group report projected that the population density in Bihar which was 881 per km in 2001 as against the all-India average of 313, would touch 1,038 per sq km by 2011 as compared to the all-India average of 365. By 2026, Bihar's population density will touch 1,209 per sq km as compared the all-India average of 426.

The 2011 Census delivers a shock. The population of Bihar is 103.8 million in 2011 as against the projection of 97.72 million. Bihar has reached the population projections made for 2016 in 2011 itself. In terms of population density, the 2011 figures for Bihar are 1,039 per sq km as against the projection of 977 per sq km. However, a modest redeeming fact is that despite such slippages in the population targets, the urban ratio in Bihar in 2011 stands at 11.3 per cent as against the Expert Committee's projection of 10.5 per cent.

Table 4.2

Proportion (Percentage) Urban Population to Total Population (2011-2026): Projection by the GoI Expert Committee

	2001	*2011*	*2021*	*2026*
Andhra Pradesh	27.3	27.7	28.1	34.0
Bihar	10.5	10.5	10.6	11.6
Gujarat	37.4	40.3	43.4	53.0
Haryana	28.9	33.6	38.7	46.3
Karnataka	34.0	37.2	40.5	49.3
Kerala	26.0	25.5	25.1	30.3
Madhya Pradesh	26.5	27.7	28.9	34.8
Maharashtra	42.4	46.2	50.1	61.0
Orissa	15.0	16.8	18.7	21.2
Punjab	33.9	38.6	43.5	52.5
Rajasthan	23.4	23.9	24.4	29.1
Tamil Nadu	44.0	54.0	64.4	74.8
Uttar Pradesh	20.8	21.9	23.2	27.2
West Bengal	28.0	28.5	29.0	35.1
All-India	27.8	30.0	32.3	38.2

Source: GoI (2006).

4.2 Lopsided Distribution of Urbanisation across Size-Class of Cities and Districts in Bihar

The ADB report (2008) states, 'according to the 2001 census, Bihar had an urban population of only 8.68 million, or 10.46 per cent of the total population, versus the national average of 28 per cent. About 60 per cent of this urban population is in the southern part of the state, with a significant concentration in Patna, and more than 50 per cent is in class I towns (towns with a population of more than 100,000; Bihar had 19 of these in the 2001 census), thus putting concentrated pressure on those towns'.

In 2001, Bihar had a total of 140 urban centres compared to 832 in Tamil Nadu, 378 in Maharashtra, 375 in West Bengal, 704 in Uttar Pradesh and 394 in Madhya Pradesh. The relative shortfall in the number of urban centres becomes much sharper when normailsed with respect to the population size of different states.

Figure 4.1

2011 Census: Density of Population (State-wise)

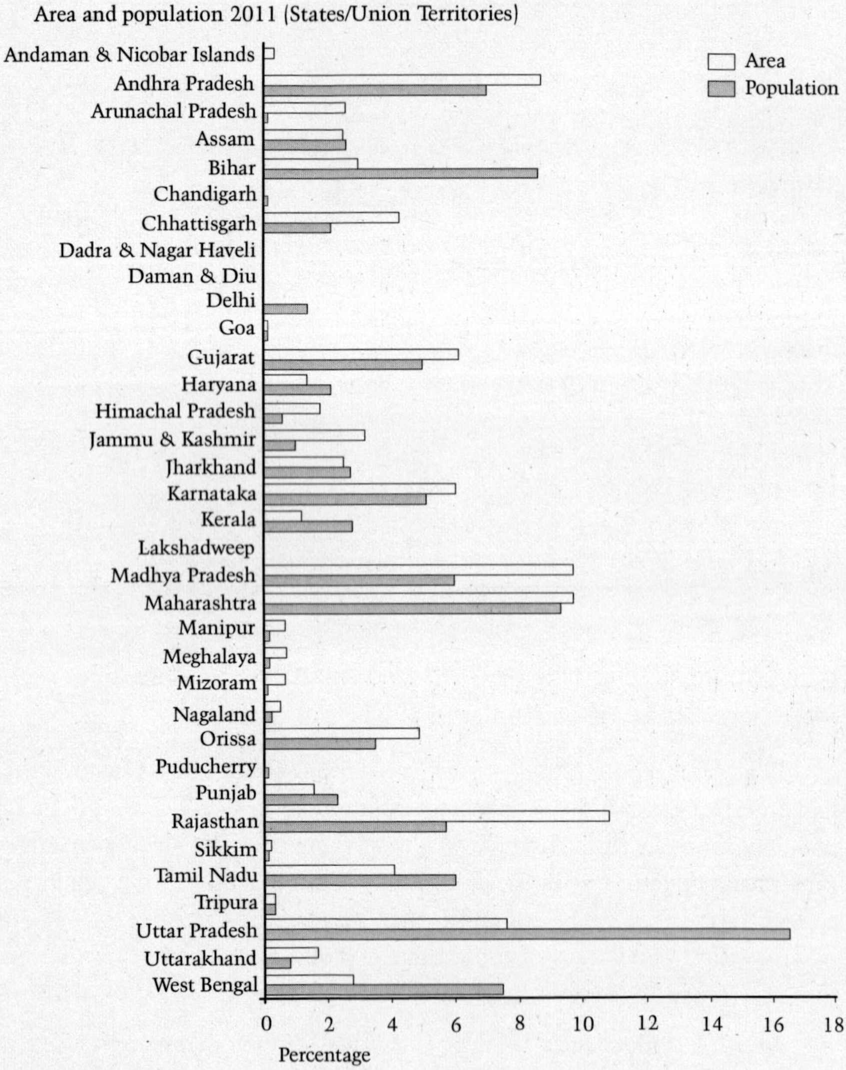

Source: GoI (2011b).

Table 4.3

Bihar: Selected Demographic Indicators District-wise (2001 and 2011)

	Population (in lakh) 2011	Rural Population(%) 2001	Density per sq km 2011	Nagar Nigam No. 2001	Nagar Parishad No. 2001	Nagar Panchayat No. 2001	Nagar Nigam Population 2001 (in lakh)	Nagar Parishad Population 2001 (in lakh)	Nagar Panchayat Population 2001 (in lakh)
Patna	57.72	58.4	1803	1	6	7	13.66	3.83	1.92
Nalanda	29.72	85.1	1220	1	1	4	2.32		1.01
Rohtas	29.62		763		2	3		2.50	0.69
Kaimur	16.29	96.8	488		1	1		0.42	0.27
Buxar	17.07	90.8	1003		2			1.29	
Bhojpur	27.2	86.1	1136	1		5	2.03		1.58
Gaya	43.79	86.3	880	1		3	3.89		0.71
Aurangabad	25.11	91.6	760		1	3		0.79	0.38
Jehanabad	11.24	91.6	1206		1	1		0.82	0.3
Arwal	6.99		1099		1	1		0.49	
Nawada	22.16	92.6	889		1	2		0.82	0.57
Saran	39.43	90.8	1493		1	6		1.79	1.84
Siwan	33.18	94.5	1495		1	2		1.10	0.39
Gopalganj	25.58	93.9	1258		1	3		0.54	0.76
Muzaffarpur	47.78	90.7	1506	1		3	3.05		0.6
Sitamarhi	34.19	94.3	1491		1	4		0.57	0.56
Sheohar	6.56	95.6	1882			1			
W. Champaran	39.22	89.8	750		3	2		2.49	0.60
E. Champaran	50.82	93.6	1281		2	8		1.50	1.68

contd...

...contd...

	Population (in lakh) 2011	*Rural Population(%) 2001*	*Density per sq km 2011*	*Nagar Nigam No. 2001*	*Nagar Parishad No. 2001*	*Nagar Panchayat No. 2001*	*Nagar Nigam Population 2001 (in lakh)*	*Nagar Parishad Population 2001 (in lakh)*	*Nagar Panchayat Population 2001 (in lakh)*
Vaishali	34.94	93.1	1717		1	2		1.19	0.67
Darbhanga	39.21	91.9	1721	1	1		2.67	0.62	
Samastipur	42.54	96.4	1465		1	2		0.62	0.48
Madhubani	44.76	96.5	1279		1	3		0.66	0.58
Saharsa	18.97	91.7	1125		1	1		1.25	0.22
Supaul	22.28	94.9	919		1	2		0.54	0.34
Madhepura	19.94	95.9	1116		1	1		0.45	0.23
Purnea	32.73	91.3	1014	1		2	2.07		0.51
Araria	28.06	93.9	992		2	1		1.01	0.30
Kishanganj	16.9	90.0	898		1	2		0.86	0.43
Katihar	30.68	90.9	1004	1	1	1	2.01		0.22
Bhagalpur	30.32	81.3	1180	1	1		3.40	0.42	0.64
Banka	20.29	96.5	672			2			0.56
Munger	13.59	72.1	958	1		1	2.14		0.27
Lakhisarai	10.00	85.3	815		1	1		0.78	0.40
Begusarai	29.54	95.4	1540	1	1	3		0.65	1.17
Jamui	17.56	92.6	567		1	1		0.67	0.37
Khagaria	16.57	94.0	1115		1	1		0.45	0.31
Sheikhpura	6.34	84.5	922		1	1		0.51	0.38
Bihar	103.8	89.5	1039	11	41	88	37.24	29.63	21.94

Note: The data in respect of the urban centres are based on 2001 Census.

Source: *Bihar Economic Survey 2010-11.*

The distribution of towns by size classes also presents an interesting picture. In Bihar, the Class I towns accounted for 14.6 per cent of the total number of urban centres, while the share of Class III plus IV towns was 70.8 per cent. In Tamil Nadu, the share of Class I towns was just 3.1 per cent while Class III plus IV towns which are closest to the rural areas, accounted for 90.2 per cent of the total. In Maharashtra, West Bengal, Uttar Pradesh and Madhya Pradesh, the shares of Class III plus IV towns were 87.06, 76.8, 84.52 and 77.78 per cent respectively. This gives a picture of the relative deprivation in rural-urban linkages in Bihar.

Table 4.3 above presents the district-wise distribution of urban centres in Bihar. It shows the extent of deprivation in urban centres across the majority of districts in Bihar. Many districts have just one *nagar parishad* with a population of around 0.5 lakh and one or two *nagar panchayats*, each with an average population size of 0.2 to 0.3 lakh. This scenario has not only affected the quality of life in the urban centres of these districts but badly impacted the rural hinterland in terms of human development services and commercial linkages.

That the urban areas of Bihar have not served their role as engines of growth is clearly illustrated by the following migration patterns.

Table 4.4

Lifetime Net Migration Rate per 100 Population in Rural and Urban Areas by Sex (2001) (PoB Criteria)

States	*Total*		*Rural*		*Urban*	
	Males	*Females*	*Males*	*Females*	*Males*	*Females*
Andhra Pradesh	-0.78	-0.8	-0.13	-0.07	-2.48	-2.76
Bihar	-7	-2.35	-1.47	0.99	-52.92	-31.92
Gujarat	3.27	1.31	1.32	0.34	6.42	2.99
Haryana	4.44	4.33	3.39	4.01	6.99	5.11
Karnataka	0.44	0.04	0.18	-0.04	0.95	0.21
Kerala	-2.72	-2.37	0.26	0.17	-11.21	-9.63
Madhya Pradesh	0.18	0.39	-0.36	-0.47	1.67	2.8
Orissa	-1.21	-0.43	-0.23	-0.2	-6.52	-1.82
Punjab	1.16	-0.42	0.27	-0.13	2.86	-0.99
Rajasthan	-2.15	-1.44	-0.11	0.03	-8.69	-6.37
Tamil Nadu	-1.59	-1.44	-0.95	-0.96	-2.4	-2.05
Uttar Pradesh	-4.99	-3.12	-0.67	-0.2	-21.22	-14.44
West Bengal	1.41	0.43	0.24	-0.11	4.33	1.87

Note: PoB—Place of Birth.

Source: Singh (2009).

Table 4.4 shows that the outmigration rates from Bihar were higher than other states by several multiples. This is a well known fact. But what may come as a surprise to many are the enormously high net outmigration rates from the urban areas of Bihar.

4.3 Urban Policy, Reforms and Programmes

There appears to be a 'blind spot' with respect to the critical issue of stunted urbanisation. Given the preponderantly rural nature of the population in the state and the high rural poverty ratio, the development discourse in Bihar seems to focus almost exclusively on rural stagnation. The abysmally low rate of urbanisation in Bihar and its skewed character are seen mainly as a symptom of rural stagnation. Thus, while one hears of some hues and cries on the dismal state of urbanisation in Bihar, and of late, some remedial measures have been launched, this vital pillar of transformation has not received the attention that it deserves in the state's inclusive growth agenda.

ADB which has initiated some work in the urban sector in the state concludes, 'the state has yet to prepare a statement of its urban policy or strategy. Without such a unified policy document, urban sector works have been fragmentary and have been undertaken by different agencies without close alignment of resources, resulting in grossly inadequate and inefficient urban development...' (ADB, 2008).

There is a need to bring distributed urbanisation on the policy agenda as inclusive development on the desired scale will not be possible without it. Infact, in the absence of orderly movement along the rural-urban progression, the overall high growth rates fuelled largely by a spurt in consumption demand is likely to wane-off. The warning signals in this regard are loud and clear.

Urban-Rural Linkages: Evidence Base

Policymakers need to note the evidence emerging from some important recent studies. Based on an in-depth study of long-term trends, Datt and Ravallion (2010) of the World Bank conclude, 'a new finding from our latest research is that the post-reform period has seen a marked change in the relative importance of urban versus rural economic growth. Prior to the reform period, urban economic growth helped reduce urban poverty but brought little or no overall benefit to the rural poor; the main driving force for overall poverty reduction was rural economic growth. The picture looks different after 1991...as before, urban growth reduced urban poverty, and rural growth reduced rural poverty in the post-1991 period. But we find much stronger evidence of a positive feedback effect from urban economic growth to rural poverty reduction than we had found in the pre-1991 data'.

Similarly, another recent study concludes that galvanising small towns may serve both urban and rural poverty reduction objectives (Himanshu *et al.*, 2010).

As indicated in Chapter 1, the most conclusive evidence regarding the impact of urban-rural linkages on the rural baseline in India comes from Krishna and Vajpai (2011).

This study notes, 'globalisation-driven economic growth in a country whose population remains largely rural has spatial effects on the distribution of benefits...A combination of spatial dispersion and global integration has created a new strategic role for major cities... [which] now function in four new ways: first, as highly concentrated command points in the organization of the economy; second, as key locations for finance and for specialised service firms, which have replaced manufacturing as the leading economic sectors; third, as sites of production...; and fourth, as markets for the products and innovations produced...The post-liberalisation Indian experience mimics these trends, showing how growth that is services-driven and globally-linked spreads downward in lineal linkage from bigger towns to smaller settlements' (Ibid.).

This study categorises rural areas located adjacent to towns within a distance of 5 kms as the 'umbra' and affirms that this population segment (constituting 13.1 per cent of the rural Indian population according to the Census of 2001) has benefited from national growth during the post-liberalisation period. 'Every income quintile in umbra villages increased its purchasing power, with the richest groups experiencing the largest, and the poorest groups experiencing the smallest, percentage increase' (Ibid.).

Villages outside the five kilometer perimeter have been categorised as the 'penumbra'. Within the 'penumbra', villages located between 5 and 10 kilometers from the nearest town accounted for 19.5 per cent of the rural population in 2001 and villages beyond 10 kilometers from the nearest town accounted for 67.5 per cent of the entire rural population. 'In penumbra villages, as well, the richest groups grew richer, albeit not to the same extent as the richest groups in umbra villages. However, every other quintile has become poorer than before. The poorest groups in penumbra villages have seen their purchasing power fall by more than one-sixth over the same 12-year period' (Ibid.).

'Poverty has been reduced within umbra villages, but it has simultaneously increased within penumbra villages...in villages located between five and 10 kilometers from the nearest town, the percentage in poverty went up by 5.6 per cent over this 12-year period, while still further away, more than 10 kilometers from towns, the increase in poverty was higher, 6.2 per cent. The sorriest part is that the vast majority of rural Indians live within such penumbra villages, more than five kilometers from the nearest town...More than 95 per cent of the rural populations of Andhra Pradesh, Orissa, and Jharkhand, and more than 90 per cent of the rural populations of Bihar, West Bengal and Chhattisgarh, live in villages located more than five kilometers from the nearest town. These people have seen their purchasing power drop, even as the country as a whole has grown rapidly. That they might experience discontent and disenchantment becomes easier to fathom' (Ibid.).

'Instead of being mitigated, these disadvantages of distance have been compounded by public policies. Critical infrastructure has been located preferentially in close-to-urban villages...Consequently, people in further away villages have faced a harder time in making connections with market-based opportunities' (Ibid.).

The study draws attention to three contemporary trends to explain why rural assets and incomes are both patterned radically differently in the villages in the umbra and in the penumbra, the nature of the handicaps suffered by the penumbra villagers and why distance to town matters so much?

First, is that villages closer to towns have been able to leverage better supplementary incomes from the non-agricultural sources during this period of decline in the amounts received per capita from agriculture (both in relative and absolute value) as a result of slow agricultural growth and a preponderance of tiny and uneconomic family plots due to sub-division of land holdings with each passing generation. 'While people of the lowest quintile in umbra villages—because of their proximity to towns and assisted by superior infrastructure—have been able to avail themselves of non-agricultural labour opportunities (in addition to undertaking agricultural labour in their villages), the lowest income quintile in villages beyond 10 kilometers from the nearest town have had to rely more centrally on agricultural labour, thus limiting their earning potential...relatively richer villagers have increased their holds on the most lucrative urban opportunities, arising from salaried and professional occupations' (Ibid.).

Second, is the differential provision of critical infrastructure. Between 1991 and 2001, 'the percentage of villages connected by paved roads went up from 42 per cent to 64 per cent, and the proportion served with electric power went up from 68 per cent to 76 per cent. But such growth was disproportionately located in umbra (or inner-circle) villages...While 67 per cent of villages within five kilometers of towns were connected by paved roads in 2001, the corresponding proportions in villages 21-30 kilometers and more than 50 kilometers from towns were much smaller, 49 per cent and 34 per cent, respectively. Similarly, while more than 84 per cent of umbra villages were served by power supply, this proportion fell to 59 per cent in villages located furthest from towns. Poorer roads and greater distance working together considerably raise the transaction costs that have to be incurred by people from penumbra villages' (Ibid.).

Third, 'the rising premium to higher education and superior skills, the preferential location of high schools and colleges in towns and villages closer to towns (and the greater ability of richer villagers to acquire higher education (no matter at what distance), helps explain further the growing gap between richer and poorer villagers and among villages located closer to and further from towns...the proportion of households in which one or more adults have secondary or higher falls from 48 per cent in the nearest villages to 35 per cent in villages at the greatest radial distance from towns. In each band of village, however, this proportion is, not surprisingly, greatest among the highest income groups. Differences in educational ability are related to the ease of access that people in nearer and further villages have to high schools and colleges... As recently as 2008, DLHS-3 data show, people from penumbra villages needed to travel, on average, 12 kilometers in order to attend higher secondary schools, more than twice the distance that umbra villagers needed to travel for the same purposes. The difference in distance to college between umbra and penumbra villages is also large and significant: 12 kilometers vs 22 kilometers' (Ibid.).

While according to this study, the proportion of rural population in umbra villages could have increased from 13 per cent in 2001 to 31 per cent in 2008 and the proportion living in the furthest-out villages (more than 10 kilometers from the nearest town) may have fallen even more drastically (by as much as 25 percentage points), the authors are not hopeful that the autonomous growth of markets, and with it, the spread of towns, will bring progressively more villagers within the beneficial inner circle. The study concludes, 'unfortunately, the data do not support any such optimistic prognosis. While towns have, in fact, advanced, the bad news is that towns have gone where market forces have taken them, following the money, while largely avoiding marginal areas with greater concentrations of poorer people. In 2008, for example, villages beyond five kilometers of towns accounted for 69 per cent of the entire rural population, but even greater proportions of poorer people—more than 75 per cent of scheduled castes, 83 per cent of scheduled tribes and 73 per cent of below-poverty-line households—lived within such villages. It seems too much to hope that the expansion of towns in the future will automatically correct these trends' (Ibid.).

The study concludes, 'the question of exclusion of many has to be addressed. Unless investments in high-quality physical and social infrastructure are simultaneously made that connect outlying areas with the mainstream of growth, inequality will continue growing, and inclusive growth will remain a distant dream...Currently, too little is being done in this regard in India, and as a result, "in terms of inequality of opportunity and intergenerational mobility", India may well be on the way to becoming "one of the worst [countries] in the world" (Bardhan, 2010: 132)' (Ibid.).

The Navodaya Shahar model shows a feasible strategy for creating high-quality physical and social infrastructure in the penumbra, particularly in the context of Bihar and other backward regions/districts in the country which are predominantly rural. It argues that multiplying rapidly the number of medium and small towns or creating economic and social infrastructure of the desired quality across the vast rural expanse of Bihar are not likely to materialise in the medium term. Also, the usual public agency-led approach to infrastructure creation and provision of services is not going to address suitably the needs of the vast ranks of the assetless. In such scenarios, an approach based on the 'triple bottom line' of the poor could provide the initial impetuous in the penumbra. Laying down this foundation will begin to dissolve the strong distance-bias that Krishna and Bajpai (2011) refers to, and also set the base for an inclusive urban-rural integration process. This will help reverse the current trend of growing disparity and often immiserisation as a result of growth and urbanisation that Krishna and Bajpai (2011) alludes to with strong evidence.

Urban Reforms and Programmes

In the last few years, the state government has launched a number of urban reform initiatives and measures to boost investment in urban infrastructure. The website of the state's Urban Development and Housing Department provides the following overview.

Box 4.1

Progress in the Urban Reform Agenda in Bihar (As Reported by the State Government)

- Effective implementation of decentralisation initiatives as envisaged in 74th CAA.
- Urban Land (Ceiling and Regulation) Act has been repealed in August 2006.
- The Apartment Ownership Act which had severe shortcomings, restricting investment in the sector, has been amended in August 2006.
- Reform of Rent Control/Municipal Law has been finalised. To be placed before the Assembly in the winter session.
- Rationalisation of stamp duty—brought down from the existing 18 per cent to 10 per cent in May 2006, with a target to reach 5 per cent.
- Bye-laws have been revised in May 2006 to streamline the approval process for construction of buildings.
- In order to attract investment in multiplexes and malls, building bye-laws, cinema rules have been amended in August 2006.
- Building bye-laws have been amended in April 2006 to incorporate structural safety norms, rainwater harvesting and provision for disabled persons, etc.
- State government has computerised registration of land and property, and property title certification.
- In several ULBs, public-private participation projects have been experimented starting with garbage disposal, street lighting, construction of bus stands, etc.
- Introduction of a system of e-governance using IT application for various urban services and reform of property tax.
- Master Plans and GIS mapping of major towns have been taken up.
- Training of women councillors is going on through the Regional Centres for Urban and Environmental Studies (RCUES), Lucknow. About 25 per cent women councillors in the state have already been trained.
- Emphasis on creating and augmenting basic infrastructure facilities in water supply, sewerage, storm water drainage, solid waste management, roads and bridges in all the 122 ULBs in the State.

Source: Website of the state's Urban Development and Housing Department *(http://urban.bih.nic.in/.)*

The *Bihar Economic Survey 2010-11* highlights the following programmes in the urban sector:

- Twenty-one towns along the river Ganga have been taken up under National Ganga River Basin Authority (NGRBA) project for improvement in facilities. The interventions envisaged are: (i) comprehensive sewerage and related projects; (ii) riverfront development in Patna; and (iii) integrated solid waste management projects and the Mukti Dham Yojana. A society is proposed to be formed to implement and monitor the NGRBA projects, along with other projects related to environmental protection of Ganga River. For this, the nodal agency designated is the Urban Development and Housing Department (UDHD).
- The state government has started work under Water Supply Scheme in 26 urban local bodies (ULBS) with an outlay of Rs 315 crore. Under basic services to urban poor (BSUP), 15,748 houses have been sanctioned for construction in 21 towns at an estimated cost of Rs 833.31 crore.
- Improvement of water supply for the ULBs of Patna, Phulwari Sharif, Khagaul and Bodhgaya was initiated in 2009-10 for which a sum of Rs 498.39 crore was approved.
- Some initiatives have been taken for the solid waste management in the state which includes the preparation of Draft Project Proposals (DPPs), contracts for collection and transportation of waste, monitoring of compost plants and landfill sites, identification of landfill sites etc.

The state government has also drawn on international cooperation in pursuit of its urban development agenda. An example is the Samvardhan programme, which is a six-year partnership programme (2010-2016) between the Government of Bihar and the United Kingdom's Department for International Development (DFID, UK). The programme aims to significantly enhance the ability of identified ULBs to provide urban services and attract private investment in the state. The programme will cover 28 urban centres that are expected to become hubs for economic activities and thereby benefitting the wider state.

However, a comparison across states in the context of the programmes of the Central Government for urban development, urban services and urban poverty alleviation shows that Bihar has lagged seriously behind others in terms of accessing this key resource. The extremely low coverage of Class III and Class VI and V towns is a matter of particular concern as unlike states such as Punjab, the state government in Bihar is not in a position to allocate suitable funds to these out of its own resources.

Table 4.5

*Class-wise Distribution of the Towns/Cities (State-wise) Yet to be Covered by JNNURM and UIDSSMT for 15 Major States (Census 2001)**

States	*Class of Towns*	*Percentage of Population Yet to be Covered*	*Total No. of Cities/Towns*	*No of Cities/Towns Yet to be Covered*
1	*2*	*3*	*4*	*5*
Andhra Pradesh	Class I	25.39	47	30
	Class II	61.70	52	32
	Class III-IV	58.91	111	65
Assam	Class I	34.91	6	4
	Class II	77.40	7	6
	Class III-IV	75.25	112	82
Bihar	Class I	62.56	19	17
	Class II	86.69	19	17
	Class III-IV	87.90	92	80
Gujarat	Class I	16.56	27	17
	Class II	59.39	36	22
	Class III-IV	73.97	179	135
Haryana	Class I	65.41	20	16
	Class II	100.00	7	7
	Class III-IV	93.81	79	75
Karnataka	Class I	34.00	30	22
	Class II	78.16	28	22
	Class III-IV	80.77	212	173
Kerala	Class I	36.47	10	7
	Class II	80.72	24	19
	Class III-IV	81.66	125	102
Madhya Pradesh	Class I	43.11	25	19
	Class II	90.25	26	23
	Class III-IV	93.00	343	315

contd...

...contd...

1	2	3	4	5
Maharashtra	Class I	14.50	40	23
	Class II	65.79	44	29
	Class III-IV	77.52	294	234
Orissa	Class I	46.33	9	6
	Class II	72.29	15	13
	Class III-IV	85.48	114	94
Punjab	Class I	43.08	14	10
	Class II	93.63	18	17
	Class III-IV	91.04	125	114
Rajasthan	Class I	62.00	19	17
	Class II	91.12	27	25
	Class III-IV	76.06	176	136
Tamil Nadu	Class I	9.60	26	18
	Class II	80.84	56	46
	Class III-IV	83.31	750	634
Uttar Pradesh	Class I	44.06	54	40
	Class II	84.27	55	47
	Class III-IV	89.80	595	531
West Bengal	Class I	5.67	58	7
	Class II	93.03	29	27
	Class III-IV	91.16	288	269
All-India	Class I	24.08	441	315
	Class II	79.22	496	396
	Class III-IV	84.02	4224	3496

*Note:** As on September 2009.
JNNURM - Jawaharlal Nehru National Urban Renewal Mission.
UIDSSMT - Urban Infrastructure Development Scheme for Small and Medium Towns.
Source: Kundu and Samanta (2011).

The position in respect of funds release under JNNURM and UIDSSMT presented below captures the neglect of this sector over the years at the level of policymakers in the state. It also partly reflects the kind of treatment that the state has received from the Central Government.

The breakup of per capita spending by the Central Government shows that the relative gap for Bihar is higher in so far as programmes for the smaller towns are concerned (Kundu and Samanta, 2011).

A report on Bihar by the concerned Advisor in the Planning Commission (available on the Commission's website) sums up the situation. It concludes, 'if Sarva Siksha Abhiyan (SSA) is one of the better implemented flagship programmes in the state, implementation of JNNURM appears to be on the other end of the spectrum. There is a need for a special Task Force for monitoring the implementation of flagship and other important programmes.'

Table 4.6

Funds Released to Allocations under Urban Development Schemes (JNNURM + UIDSSMT)

States	*Funds Released Compared to Allocation (%)*
Andhra Pradesh	87.87
Bihar	25.9
Gujarat	49.67
Haryana	53.62
Karnataka	44.11
Kerala	44.13
Madhya Pradesh	46.62
Maharashtra	51.45
Orissa	63.71
Punjab	25.61
Rajasthan	51.2
Tamil Nadu	41.41
Uttar Pradesh	36.52
West Bengal	26.3
All-India	45.5

Note: * As on September 2009.
Source: Kundu and Samanta (2011).

4.4 Conclusion

The Eleventh Five Year Plan notes, 'urbanisation is a key indicator of economic development and should be seen as a positive factor for overall development... Indian cities will be the locus and engine of economic growth over the next two decades, and the realisation of an ambitious goal of 9 per cent-10 per cent growth in GDP depends fundamentally on making Indian cities much more livable, inclusive, bankable, and competitive' (GoI, 2008). But surprisingly, this dictum is rarely considered as relevant in the context of Bihar.

Table 4.7

*State-wise Annual Per Capita Spending (Rs) by the Central Government on Different Components of Urban Development Schemes Meant for Mission and Non-Mission Cities/Towns since 6 December 2005**

States	*UIG JNNURM*	*UIG UIDSSMT*	*BSUP JNNURM*	*IHSDP UIDSSMT*	*JNNURM (UIG+ BSUP)*	*UIDSSMT (UIG+ IHSDP)*	*UIG (JNNURM+ UIDSSMT)*	*Pro-Poor Component (JNNURM+ UIDSSMT)*	*Urban Schemes Total (JNNURM+ UIDSSMT)*
Andhra Pradesh	190.61	266.96	155.32	85.69	345.93	352.66	230.93	118.55	349.48
Arunachal Pradesh	2205.58	153.63	430.01	0	2635.59	153.63	548.95	82.84	631.79
Assam	161.25	77.28	82.35	21.92	243.6	99.2	98.79	37.4	136.19
A&N Islands	0	0	0	93.32	0	93.32	0	93.32	93.32
Bihar	96.55	35.91	76.57	20.85	173.13	56.75	51.41	35.1	86.51
Chandigarh	44.43	0	225.61	0	270.04	0	44.43	225.61	270.04
Chhattisgarh	324.74	38.57	208.68	48.88	533.42	87.45	89.05	77.07	166.12
D & Nagar Haveli	0	4.74	0	4.2	0	8.94	2.94	22.98	25.92
Daman and Diu	0	11.07	0	10.36	0	21.43	4.74	4.2	8.94
Delhi	2.94	0	22.98	0	25.92	0	11.07	10.36	21.43
Goa	0	0	26.43	0	26.43	0	0	26.43	26.43
Gujarat	170.36	70.14	69.24	35.94	239.6	106.08	133.89	57.12	191.02
Haryana	172.28	26.55	34.18	41.45	206.46	68	57.58	39.91	97.49
Himachal Pradesh	265.73	39.19	61.65	87.01	327.38	126.2	97.66	80.47	178.13
Jammu and Kashmir	136.12	416.94	38.98	91.02	175.1	507.96	216.17	53.81	269.98
Jharkhand	76.59	32.02	27.23	32.89	103.83	64.91	56.87	29.74	86.61

contd...

...contd...

States	*UIG JNNURM*	*UIG UIDSSMT*	*BSUP JNNURM*	*IHSDP UIDSSMT*	*JNNURM (UIG+ BSUP)*	*UIDSSMT (UIG+ IHSDP)*	*UIG (JNNURM+ UIDSSMT)*	*Pro-Poor Component (JNNURM+ UIDSSMT)*	*Urban Schemes Total (JNNURM+ UIDSSMT)*
Karnataka	150.63	57.57	29.72	21.95	180.36	79.52	95.12	25.09	120.21
Kerala	140.93	70.43	68.23	37.26	209.17	107.68	91.2	46.38	137.58
Madhya Pradesh	157.57	58.6	50.72	18.01	208.29	76.61	88.44	27 87	116.31
Maharashtra	181.54	148.83	74.1	77.31	255.64	226.14	169.39	75.29	244.68
Manipur	94.4	228.44	89.53	85.58	183.93	314.02	161.94	87.54	249.48
Meghalaya	389.22	77.52	127.23	134.73	516.45	212.25	265.25	130.21	395.46
Mizoram	29.29	91.11	155.04	193.87	184.33	284.98	52.34	169.51	221.85
Nagaland	128.18	0	1191.03	278.93	1319.22	278.93	37.48	545.65	583.13
Orissa	334.16	42.32	28.23	41.1	362.4	83.41	95.63	38.75	134.38
Punjab	110.35	57.1	7.07	5.84	117.43	62.93	73.81	6.23	80.03
Pondicherry	194.15	0	79.79	31.52	273.94	31.52	145.6	67.72	213.33
Rajasthan	237.43	61.17	26.37	35.38	263.8	96.55	106.4	33.07	139.47
Sikkim	794.08	1,031.74	535.59	0	1329.67	1031.74	928.49	232.69	1161.18
Tamil Nadu	138.69	54.38	74.68	20.06	213.37	74.44	80.97	37.29	118.26
Tripura	195.54	207.85	77.51	69.45	273.05	277.31	203.63	72.22	275.85
Uttar Pradesh	130.04	41.26	60.75	23.12	190.79	64.38	68.98	34.87	103.86
Uttarakhand	136.38	37.59	16.78	2.21	153.17	39.79	75.95	7.87	83.82
West Bengal	61.09	63.49	70.66	124.22	131.75	187.71	61.88	88.24	150.12
All-India	153.3	78.33	66.25	40.38	219.55	118.71	112.85	52.3	165.15

Note: UIG - Urban Infrastructure and Governance.
BSUP - Basic Services to the Urban Poor.
IHSDP - Integrated Housing and Slum Development Programme.
* = As on September 2009.

Source: Kundu and Samanta (2011).

Policymakers, at both the state and the Central levels, need to wake up to the reality that the relationship between rural stagnation and stunted urbanisation in Bihar has not been a one-way causality. Particularly, remedial measures need to be planned in light of the highly gloomy picture that emerges from the projections of the Technical Group on Population Projections Constituted by the National Commission on Population (GoI, 2006). The results of the 2011 Census deliver a stern warning that things may move further in the wrong direction.

There is a need to pay special attention to rejuvenating and expanding the small and medium towns that constitute the cutting edge of rural-urban linkages.

Yet, it is also important to accept that given the humungous backlog, these measures will not be able to meet the needs of the vast rural masses. Further, given the high cost of land even in small towns and urban centres, it is unlikely that the rural poor will be able to find berth. Thus, Bihar will have to chart out its own model that goes beyond the conventional urbanisation modality.

The Navodaya Shahar model responds to this challenge. It seeks to create conditions in rural hinterland such that the benefits of urban services and livelihoods are realised while maintaining close functional connectivity with the countryside. Most important, this model will provide an opportunity to create and distribute to masses wealth that normally ensues from an inclusive urbanisation process.

5 Outmigration and Implications for Inclusive Growth Strategies in Bihar

5.1 Bihar and Migration

The words 'Bihar' and 'migration' are indelibly linked, so much so that in many of the constituencies located thousands of miles away from Bihar, it is a hot political agenda. In some places, politicians make all-out effort to woo the significant 'Bihari' vote bank. Thus during elections, blaring *Bhojpuri* song is a common sound in the peri-urban areas of Delhi. In some others regions, 'Bihari' bashing to whip up local jingoism is seen as a quick route to political stardom.

But back in the home state, this vast multitude remains faceless and voiceless despite the fact that its back-bending work is fuelling the hearth in one-third to one-half of the households in rural Bihar. The conditions at the point of origin remain such that very little of their income is converted into productive assets—physical and human. The vicious cycle spins on.

The migrant population, their income and skill base, constitute an important leverage for transformational strategies underlying the Navodaya Shahar model. This chapter outlines the trends and pattern in outmigration from Bihar and attempts to unravel its implications for inclusive growth strategies in the state, and particularly for making the proposed Navodaya Shahar model a reality.

5.2 Trends in Outmigration from Bihar

The following analysis draws on the NSS data from the 64th Round (July 2007-June 2008) as well as some excellent recent studies capturing rich details of this human endeavour. The latter include: Kumar and Banerjee, 2010 of IIPA and Bhaskaran and Mehta, 2010 of IHD. The IHD study was prepared for the South Asia Network of Economic Research Institutes (SANEI). The IIPA study was sponsored by the Government of Bihar.

According to the NSS 64th Round data, 25.8 per cent of the rural households in Bihar reported outmigration in 2007-08. The corresponding figure for urban Bihar was 16.8 per cent.

Table 5.1

Proportion (per 1,000) of Households Reporting Outmigration

State	*No. of Households Reporting Outmigration per 1,000 Households*	
	Rural	*Urban*
Andhra Pradesh	267	173
Bihar	258	168
Gujarat	300	193
Haryana	412	324
Karnataka	276	133
Kerala	509	438
Madhya Pradesh	243	162
Maharashtra	354	200
Orissa	285	185
Punjab	274	153
Rajasthan	374	286
Tamil Nadu	233	154
Uttar Pradesh	391	235
West Bengal	311	231
All-India	304	193

Source: NSSO (2010c).

Other studies report much higher outmigration rates from Bihar. The IIPA study estimates that migration of labour from Bihar may be affecting about one-third of the rural households. These ratios are much higher in some districts (Purnia–48.2%, Araria–53.2%, Gaya–44.2% and Munger–44.2%) (Kumar and Banerji, 2010).

The IHD study which traces migration from the Samastipur district of Bihar to Delhi concludes, 'in the sample population, one out of every three people had migrated to Delhi, indicating a high incidence of migration. Two out of three people who belonged to economically active age group (14-44 years) migrated, indicating a major imbalance in the supply or availability of able bodied' (Bhaskaran and Mehta, 2010).

An earlier study (Karan, 2003 cited in Deshingkar, *et al.*, 2006) covering districts in north Bihar showed a phenomenal increase in migration rates from 28 per cent to 49 per cent in a 17-year period. This study noted that all caste groups, as well as Muslims migrate and the recent increase has been most marked among OBCs, SCs and Muslims.

5.3 Composition of Outmigrants and Factors Affecting Outmigration

The IIPA study reported that the OBC and EBC social groups combined accounted for 55 per cent of the migrant population while the share of the SC communities was around 21 per cent. The IHD study found that 34.7 per cent of the migrants belonged to SC communities, 44.3 per cent belong to OBCs, and the balance 20 per cent were from the general category. This indicates that people from disadvantaged groups are more likely to migrate.

The above social composition of migrants found its reflection in the occupational pattern of the migrating population. The IHD study found that 71.7 per cent of the migrant households were casual labourers—39.3 per cent were agriculture labourers while 32.4 per cent were non-agriculture labourers. Rest of them were small and marginal cultivators (14.2%), small traders (5.5%), salaried (3%), or in traditional occupations (2%).

The role of the occupational pattern in triggering migration becomes clearer when one compares the migrant and the non-migrant population on this dimension. The IHD study reported that in the migrant population, 40.9 per cent of the households were engaged as labourers as against 15.6 per cent amongst the non-migrant population. The ratio of self-employed among the migrants was 16.95 per cent as compared to 12.2 per cent among the non-migrants. Students constituted nearly 30 per cent of the non-migrant population, while their share in the migrant population was nearly half, at 16.4 per cent.

The IHD study also found close relationship between the size of landholding and the probability of migration. Nearly 96 per cent of the outmigrants belonged to the landless (55%) and marginal landholder (41%) categories.

The IIPA study found that whereas 81 per cent of the non-migrant households reported owning land, 61 per cent of the migrant households reported nil or negligible land ownership. This study makes a further important point based on differential land productivity. The reported average earning from crops among non-migrants was higher in all the districts for which the IIPA study collected data. Given that the intensity of cropping was higher for non-migrants in only half of the districts covered, this study concluded that there is a possibility of the non-migrant families possessing better land that allows them to go in for higher value crops or generates higher yields.

Age-wise analysis indicates that 70.5 per cent of the migrants belong to the active working category of 15-44 years.

Table 5.2

Profile of Respondents

(in percentage)

Sector	*Age Group*					*Gender*		*Marital Status*		*Religious Composition*		
	<20	*20-30*	*30-40*	*40-50*	*>50*	*Male*	*Female*	*Married*	*Not Married*	*H*	*M*	*C*
Rural	7.78	56.11	27.22	4.44	4.44	96.11	3.89	76.67	23.33	92.2	6.67	-
Urban	6.43	42.14	35.24	12.86	3.33	95.48	4.52	82.14	17.86	90.5	7.86	0.48
Total	6.83	46.33	32.83	10.33	3.67	95.67	4.33	80.5	19.5	91	7.5	0.33

Note: (H=Hindu, M=Muslim, C=Christian).

Source: Kumar and Banerji (2010).

5.4 Reasons for Outmigration

Table 5.3 presents the NSS data on outmigration of 'rural males' and 'urban males' respectively. This analysis focusses on males because of the finding that women primarily migrate on account of marriage.

Table 5.3 shows that employment-related reasons account for about 88 per cent of the male outmigration from rural Bihar and 82 per cent of the outmigration from urban Bihar. In the case of urban males, education also emerges as a factor for outmigration and accounts for 11.2 per cent of the total outmigration. The NSS data broadly corresponds with the findings of other studies.

Table 5.3

Distribution (per 1,000) of Outmigrants by Reason for Outmigration (State-wise)

States	*Male (Rural)*			*Male (Urban)*		
	Employment-related Reasons	*Studies*	*Others*	*Employment-related Reasons*	*Studies*	*Others*
Andhra Pradesh	621	239	140	593	288	119
Bihar	881	25	94	822	112	66
Gujarat	733	103	164	600	215	185
Haryana	704	65	231	680	185	135
Karnataka	763	132	105	797	113	90
Kerala	735	53	212	698	70	232
Madhya Pradesh	702	129	169	772	148	80
Maharashtra	731	114	155	590	160	250
Orissa	872	45	83	775	149	76
Punjab	831	59	110	598	193	209
Rajasthan	802	81	117	694	163	143
Tamil Nadu	844	93	63	851	87	62
Uttar Pradesh	825	44	131	747	136	117
West Bengal	894	32	74	734	50	216
All-India	799	78	123	710	143	147

Source: NSSO (2010c).

The studies by IIPA and IHD throw light on the occupational structure of migrants at the point of destination. The IHD study indicates that in their origin village more than half of the respondents were engaged in agriculture-related activities (38% as casual labour in agriculture, 6% as cultivators and 5% in agriculture-related small business). In Delhi, nearly 30 per cent of the migrants started as casual labourers in construction and other non-agriculture activities, and nearly 20 per cent worked as labourers in factories. Twelve per cent became rickshaw pullers in Delhi. However, 15 per cent entered salaried jobs as office/shop/cafeteria assistants.

5.5 Remittances

The NSS 64th Round (July 2007-June 2008) provides state-wise data on average household consumer expenditure during the last 365 days, proportion of households (per 1,000) receiving remittance and the average amount of remittance received per household during 2007-08. This data is available separately for rural and urban areas.

From Table 5.4, one key observation leaps out in the context of Bihar. This is the high proportion of households (per 1,000) receiving remittances. In rural Bihar, 192 of the 258 migrating households (per 1,000 households) received migration income (remittance) as compared to 111 households out of 304 migrating rural households (per 1,000) at the all-India level. In the case of urban Bihar, 103 households out of 168 migrating (per 1,000) received migration income. A look at the corresponding figures in comparable states further underscores the importance of migration income for rural Bihar.

Table 5.4

Remittance and Average Amount of Remittance Received per Household during 2007-08 (Rural)

State	*Average Household Consumer Expenditure during Last 365 Days per Household (Rs)*	*Average Household Consumer Expenditure during Last 365 Days per Household Receiving Remittances (Rs)*	*Proportion of Household Receiving Remittance per 1,000 Households*	*Average Amount (Rs) of Remittance Received during Last 365 Days per Household*	*Average Amount (Rs) of Remittance Received during Last 365 Days per Household Reporting Receipt of Remittance*
Andhra Pradesh	31031	30104	44	867	19892
Bihar	31913	33943	192	2907	15148
Gujarat	44531	39410	43	651	15147
Haryana	58500	68384	65	2894	44454
Karnataka	34451	36778	66	929	13977
Kerala	55746	62646	229	11719	51212
Madhya Pradesh	33205	34565	34	340	10084
Maharashtra	39429	39060	80	975	12127
Orissa	26708	31959	147	2040	13848
Punjab	62684	85016	85	7127	83527
Rajasthan	44334	49605	143	4008	28059
Tamil Nadu	30380	29567	93	2099	10084
Uttar Pradesh	39006	41694	171	2504	14677
West Bengal	32915	34591	101	1501	14877
All-India	37735	41466	111	2297	20737

Source: NSSO (2010c).

The IIPA study points to the probability of even larger proportion of the households receiving remittances. It indicates, 'almost all (99%) the migrant households stated that they received remittances from the migrant member working outside...at their destination, the proportion of respondents replying in the affirmative to the question of sending remittances to their families was 90 per cent.'

As per the NSS data, in rural Bihar, the average amount of remittances per household reporting receipt of remittances was Rs 15,148 during 2007-08. This was lower than the all-India average of Rs 20,737. For urban Bihar, the average amount of remittances per household reporting receipt of remittances was Rs 33,350 during 2007-08. This was substantially lower than the all-India average of Rs 43,589. But it may be noted that the all-India average for urban areas includes large average incomes from outmigration to other countries from states such as Punjab, Goa and Kerala.

The finding of the IIPA study which covered rural Bihar corresponds with the above NSS estimate. The IIPA study estimates the average amount received as remittances by a migrant household at Rs 15,622 annually. But according to this study, the range is quite wide—from Rs 11,346 in Khagaria to Rs 20,111 in Nawada. The IHD study indicates that on an average, a migrant remitted nearly Rs 1200-1300 per month to his village in the Samastipur district.

The IIPA study also presents the following distribution of remittances by social classes.

Table 5.5

Remittances by Different Social Groups

(in percentage)

Social Group	*<5000 (Rs)*	*5000-10000*	*10000-20000 (Rs)*	*20000-40000*	*>40000 (Rs)*	*No Answer*
ST		40	50	10		
SC	23.6	26.4	36.8	12.3	0.9	
OBC	14.0	25.6	40.4	18.4	1.2	0.4
EBC	10.3	29.3	50	8.6	1.7	
General	25.7	21.9	34.3	18.1		
Total	17.6	25.7	39.7	15.9	0.9	0.2

Source: Kumar and Banerji (2010).

Comparing the NSS data on the average remittance with the average household consumer expenditure per household receiving remittances shows that for rural Bihar, remittances accounted for 44.6 per cent of the average household consumer expenditure for these households. For urban Bihar, this works out to be 53.6 per cent.

The NSS figures on remittances to rural Bihar match with that of the IHD study which estimated that remittance constituted 47.2 per cent of the total family income.

Box 5.1

Remittances for Staying Afloat above the Poverty Line

Analysing the remittances in the context of the budget dynamics of the poor households, the IIPA study concludes, 'the average figure of Rs 15,622 turns to be extremely significant as it almost wipes out the deficit that the average migrant family faces on account of the mismatch between their expenditure and income from land and cattle.' Providing further details, the study indicates, 'to maintain the family, as per our household survey relating to expenditure, an average monthly consumption expenditure of about Rs 2500 is necessary. For an average household size of over 5, the per capita expenditure works out to be rather low, less than Rs 6000 per year, i.e. Rs 30,000 per household. This is of course the cash outflows. The cash inflows for the household from crop earnings are, on an average, less than Rs 10,000 annually. Further, income from cattle is low and the reported incidence of commercial usage of cattle is low. The income from cattle is usually less than Rs 2000 per annum. Thus the average household has a huge deficit which must be met by labour earnings.'

The IHD study highlights the fact that more than one migrant per family is needed to simply keep it afloat above the poverty line. It states, 'moreover, we may also have to correlate the average amount of remittance with the consumption which is between Rs 1200-1300 per month and Rs 14000-16000 annually. Even if the meager income earned locally by the origin household is added, it would still fall under below poverty line (BPL) level. But in the sample households, on an average two people migrated and the remittance thereof would bring them slightly above the BPL status.'

Source: Kumar and Banerji (2010) and Bhaskaran and Mehta (2010).

The IIPA study also seeks to answer a question that comes readily to mind in this MNREGA era. Nearly two-thirds of the migrants were able to remit only Rs 10,000 yearly. This comes to around less than a Rs 1,000 per month which is lower than the daily wage promised under NREGA. Thus, why are people migrating? The study concludes that they prefer to go out 'since job opportunities are in abundance and unlike NREGA it is available round the year. Second, the corruption associated with the mammoth job-guaranty scheme makes it redundant.' One of the following sub-sections explores the combination of these 'push' and 'pull' factors in some depth.

5.6 Use of Remittances

The NSS 64th Round (July 2007-June 2008) provides state-wise data on proportion of households (per 1,000) using remittance for different purposes. Such data is available for rural and urban areas separately.

An analysis of the NSS data and the field-level reality emerging from the studies mentioned above leads to some important conclusions with regard to the role that remittances are playing in the life and livelihood of migrant households in Bihar. The distinguishing feature for Bihar is that the use of remittance is oriented more towards the basic subsistence needs. Further, as brought out by the field-level studies referred to above, due to the highly dismal development baseline in the villages of origin, very little of the precious saving gets converted into productive assets—physical and human. A poignant remark in the IHD report brings this out starkly. The report states, 'many migrants mentioned that they could now afford to send their children to school rather to work. But poor school facilities resulted in drop-outs, who eventually got into some economic activity. The focused group discussions also reinstated this aspect of child labour.'

The Navodaya Shahar could provide an important avenue for asset building for migrant families. Reduction in waste and expenditure in areas such as health will supplement the resources for such asset building.

Table 5.6 presenting NSS data for rural Bihar shows that nearly 75 per cent of the households used remittances for buying food. The next in terms of importance was health care. Thirty-seven per cent of the households used remittances for health support. The expenditure on consumer durables appears to be commensurately higher. But those on education, debt repayment and saving and investment appear to be lower than the all-India average. This shows that remittances in Bihar are primarily serving subsistence-oriented consumption needs.

Table 5.6

Proportion of Households (per 1,000) Using Remittance for Specific Purpose (State-wise) (Rural)

State	*Purpose for which Remittance was Used*												
	1	*2*	*3*	*4*	*5*	*6*	*7*	*8*	*9*	*10*	*11*	*12*	*Any*
Andhra Pradesh	729	142	53	30	377	275	105	243	28	11	78	23	1000
Bihar	757	232	301	45	372	500	96	59	15	2	43	109	1000
Gujarat	749	109	211	37	404	468	88	53	8	5	79	103	1000
Haryana	714	552	295	43	431	361	57	28	28	0	80	59	1000
Karnataka	757	151	223	75	386	400	90	176	30	10	35	32	1000
Kerala	776	328	74	42	416	355	71	242	0	6	82	30	1000
Madhya Pradesh	706	279	207	52	500	337	101	54	2	3	27	49	1000
Maharashtra	734	183	146	32	454	491	75	36	24	2	49	39	1000
Orissa	741	207	185	113	210	472	160	143	12	2	49	96	1000
Punjab	660	325	270	64	212	345	110	176	24	6	133	56	1000
Rajasthan	787	312	197	53	84	481	96	150	2	4	82	85	1000
Tamil Nadu	809	186	79	35	353	420	47	299	6	2	88	22	1000
Uttar Pradesh	722	455	235	48	485	472	81	60	11	1	36	40	1000
West Bengal	817	259	197	16	360	463	127	68	4	1	52	28	1000
All-India	756	305	203	48	377	455	91	103	11	3	54	56	1000

Note: *: Use of remittances: for household consumer expenditure: on food items-01, education of household members-02, household durable-03, marriage and other ceremonies-04, health care-05, others items on household consumer expenditure-06; for improving housing condition (major repairs, purchase of land and buildings, etc.)-07, debt repayment-08, financing working capital-09, initiating new entrepreneurial activity-10, saving/investment-11, others-12.

Source: *NSS 64th Round-Migration in India: July 2007-June 2008.*

In the case of outmigrant families from urban areas, the expenditure on food is commensurately lower than the all-India average. Similarly, the expenditure on health is commensurately lower, but that on education matches the all-India average. Again as in the case of rural households, debt repayment is lower than the all-India average. The saving and investment is significantly lower than the all-India average.

The result of the IHD study shows that debt clearance ranks third in terms of the priority of households as 50 per cent of the respondents mentioned that they repaid loan. It also reports that nearly 50 per cent mentioned that they used remittance to buy agricultural land, renovate the house, used it as savings, or invested in livestock/livelihood equipment etc.

Table 5.7

Proportion of Households (per 1,000) Using Remittance for Specific Purpose (State-wise) (Urban)

State	*Purpose for which Remittance was Used*												
	1	*2*	*3*	*4*	*5*	*6*	*7*	*8*	*9*	*10*	*11*	*12*	*Any*
Andhra Pradesh	540	252	154	28	290	295	117	76	33	1	265	50	1000
Bihar	594	339	298	33	273	405	75	42	3	2	32	133	1000
Gujarat	676	233	239	32	350	505	49	32	12	5	164	69	1000
Haryana	654	431	257	30	400	403	55	22	3	0	97	64	1000
Karnataka	769	320	189	30	439	471	27	38	0	1	122	29	1000
Kerala	808	348	72	21	381	356	41	290	0	2	118	28	1000
Madhya Pradesh	703	397	293	39	351	418	40	17	2	2	106	75	1000
Maharashtra	734	347	169	31	357	430	35	48	26	1	80	54	1000
Orissa	655	219	131	74	294	355	215	157	2	0	172	57	1000
Punjab	708	278	271	64	227	372	51	47	4	5	193	101	1000
Rajasthan	783	375	151	66	137	441	53	57	8	9	157	80	1000
Tamil Nadu	716	251	147	28	419	424	63	153	14	1	207	46	1000
Uttar Pradesh	725	438	263	20	389	534	44	14	3	3	85	34	1000
West Bengal	743	271	187	61	443	399	103	59	13	1	44	45	1000
All-India	713	335	189	36	355	427	64	90	10	2	126	54	1000

Note: As in Table 5.6 above.

Source: *NSS 64th Round-Migration in India: July 2007-June 2008.*

The ODA study (Deshingkar *et al.*, 2006) also reported of attempts by households to create capital mainly by way of land. But this proportion appears to be low and confined to certain sections of the migrants. The study indicates that roughly 5-10 per cent of migrating households have been able to accumulate assets (buying, sharing in or leasing-in) through migration. These appear to be mainly OBCs who are in more remunerative work, especially "factory" work'. 'In Muzzaffarpur about 10 per cent migrants have started lease farming on 0.50-1.00 bigha land using remittances. Another 5 per cent migrants have used remittances to buy livestock, repair or upgrade their houses and set up small businesses. In Jai Nagar block, Madhubani about 15 per cent migrants use remittances for sharecropping. In Hariharpur village, Dumra block, Sitamarhi many people are investing in land' (Ibid.).

The IIPA study which has broader geographical coverage, however, presents a much more subsistence-oriented use of remittances. The proportion of households who used remittances 'solely for food' was as high as 92 per cent in Kaimur, 87 per cent in Sitamarhi and 84 per cent in Saharsa and Katihar. Nearly 75 per cent of the rural migrant workers in rural areas confirmed that food purchase was the primary use of the remittances sent by them. In the case of urban workers, in addition to essential consumption items, marriages and other ceremonies as well as house repair also emerged as important avenues for the use of remittances. An important point to note is that less than 10 per cent of the respondents reported capital expenditure in the form of purchase of land, cattle or machinery as the primary usages of remittances.

Table 5.8

Use of Remittances

District	*House Repair*	*Land Purchase*	*Cattle Purchase*	*Agri. Instrument*	*Marriage*	*Food*	*Other*	*No Response*
Katihar	0.74	1.48	2.22	5.19	4.44	83.7	2.22	
Nawada			1.48	5.19	0.74	44.44	38.52	9.63
Sitamarhi	3.7					86.67	8.15	1.48
Kaimur		0.75			0.75	91.73		6.77
Saharsa		0.74	0.74	4.44	0.74	84.44	5.93	2.96
Khagaria	0.73	0.73	3.65	6.57	21.2	23.36	39.42	4.38

Source: IIPA study.

The IHD study summarises the response of households on the impact of migration incomes. It confirms that migration incomes are mostly meeting consumption needs and those for education and health, but are making very little impact on savings and investment (see Table 5.9).

The IIPA study highlights the overall magnitude of migration incomes to bolster its case for a suitable policy on migrants and migration (see Box 5.2).

Table 5.9

Responses of Households on the Impact of Migration

	Improved Very Well	*Improved Better than Before*	*No Change*	*Got Worse*	*Total*
Impact on HH income	16.44	68.04	14.61	0.91	100
Consumption of food and essential items	5.94	74.89	19.18	0	100
Clothes and lifestyle items	3.2	68.95	27.85	0	100
Marriage/life cycle events/festivals	3.65	47.95	48.4	0	100
House renovations/maintenance	2.28	37.9	57.08	2.74	100
Alcohol/drugs/any intoxication items	2.28	10.96	75.34	11.42	100
Education	5.02	57.53	29.68	7.76	100
Health care	2.28	72.6	25.11	0	100
Entertainment	1.37	26.03	62.1	10.5	100
Durable utensils	0.46	41.55	47.03	10.96	100
Telecommunications	3.2	51.14	42.47	3.2	100
Savings	1.83	14.61	62.56	21	100

Source: IHD study.

Box 5.2

Aggregate Volume of Migration Incomes Higher than State Government Revenue

'Migration and remittances are useful to the household and also to the state. If we take the number of migrants to be 5 million, and the average annual remittances as Rs 15,000, the total value of remittances comes to Rs 7,500 crore in a year. Putting the NSDP of Bihar at Rs 1,40,000 crore (roughly) for 2009 at current prices, the contribution of remittances to Bihar's income works out to be over five per cent. Although this is not an insignificant number, it appears small in relation to the state NSDP. But the amount is more than the state government's own revenue and about 4-5 times the state's annual plan expenditure. For the poor households, the amount is invaluable as the average remittance (per household) is slightly higher than the state's per capita income.'

Source: IIPA study.

5.7 Perception on Development Requirements at the Origin

The IHD study explores the perception on development requirements at the origin in considerable depth. It reports that the respondents at both the origin and at the destination raised concerns on the lack of infrastructure in the villages and its impact on the socioeconomic development of the villages.

The respondents at the point of origin emphasised lack of schools, especially higher education facility in the village or nearby areas, lack of health care facilities and erratic or poor electricity supply.

The migrants being exposed to the life outside the state cited many other issues with regard to the conditions at the origin. These included lack of electricity to lack of industries, bank facilities, public transport systems, market for consumption goods and markets for their agricultural products. Many migrants lamented, 'if some industries or other income generating activities are established in their village they would willingly go back as Delhi was fast becoming a costly city, making migration economically non-viable.'

The IHD study presents a menu based on collation of the perspectives of migrants with regard to 'essential development services' at the origin (Table 5.10).

This menu raises questions of immense policy significance. Could the above livelihood baseline and services be met in the context of the existing village structure? Even with best of intentions, could these be achieved through an incremental and service-specific approach?

The solutions must be found early. The IHD study reports that about 67.2 per cent of origin households wanted the migrants to return to the village. Similarly, nearly two-thirds of the migrants ultimately plan to settle down in their origin village. Overall, more than half of the migrants are seeking an opportunity to return rather continuing in Delhi as the balance of 'push' and 'pull' factors alters.

Table 5.10

Changes Needed at the Origin

	Very Much Needed	*Already Exists- Access Needed to Improve*	*It can not Improve*	*Now Demanding for Change*	*Not Bothered*
Better wage for work cash payment	60	25	11	4	0
Regular employment	54	28	14	1	3
Land for cultivation	11	33	28	20	6
Better education systems	32	46	20	2	0
Better health care facility	44	34	15	7	0
Better transportation facility	51	27	17	3	2
Better communication facility	43	35	14	5	3
Better access to water/electricity	48	25	21	5	1
Social discrimination need to be stopped	44	23	27	2	4
Better entertainment facility	28	25	24	16	7

Source: Bhaskaran and Mehta (2010).

5.8 Need for Long-Term Policy on Outmigration

The migration rates seem to have peaked and levelled out. Perhaps this is a temporary phenomenon due to NREGA and the recent spurt in economic activity. But given the medium-term projection of the Expert Group on Population Projection, it is quite clear that the growing population of Bihar in the midst of frozen rural-urban ratios will continue to outmigrate in large volumes. Thus, the state needs to develop a policy that supports the migrants both at the point of destination and at the point of origin.

A number of studies have outlined measures with regard to the former aspect. These include: creation of some identity device, tracking and complaint registration system, skill development so that their earning potential improves, secure mechanisms for money transfer, increasing awareness about vulnerabilities such as HIV/AIDS etc. (Deshingkar *et al.*, 2006; Kumar and Banerji, 2010).

The Navodaya Shahar model focusses on issues at the point of origin in light of the expectations outlined in the previous sub-section. It is directly germane to the issue of systematic accumulation of assets by the migrant population. Home and garden plots and small plots for craft and trade in an organised environment will provide a secure avenue for insvestment. The low unit costs will enable even the poorer segments amongst the migrants to invest.

Quality human development services in Navodaya Shahars will not only help utilise better their hard earned income, the savings in terms of health expenditure may itself pay for the costs of transition within a few years.

Navodaya Shahars need to be planned keeping in view the picture that the migrants have painted for the niche that they wish to return to once their economic objectives have been met.

Navodaya Shahars could easily combine the 'bright city lights' (ascribed by some as the motive force behind migration) and the 'greens' of the countryside.

Conversely, the migrant population, their income, skill base and enterprise level will be an important source for creation and maturation of the Navodaya Shahars.

6 The Navodaya Shahar Model

6.1 The Navodaya Shahar Model: An Overview

The principle underlying Navodaya Shahars is 'land reform plus'. As land is not available to meet the needs of large number of landless households, the Navodaya Shahar model seeks to build a solution based on allocation of home and garden plots of 380 square metres to each landless household. This is based on the impressive evidence base advanced by FAO on the multiple benefits of homegarden plots. But the blueprint goes much further. This model argues for clustering of homegarden plots such that viable habitats are created to mount human development services, and progressively create a diversified livelihood base. Thus, this model sees Navodaya clusters as a home-grown model to compensate for the clogged land reforms agenda on the one hand, and for deficient rural-urban linkages and human development services in the vast rural expanse of Bihar on the other.

A Navodaya Shahar is visualised as a habitat of around 5,000 households to start with. This is to attain a critical minimum size for creation of quality human development services such as middle and higher secondary schools at par with the Navodaya schools and health services. The base of livelihood security provided by the home and garden plots combined with an organised framework for servicing the unmet needs of human development are expected to create a dynamic livelihood cycle. The aim is to progressively reach standards matching the vision that the migrant population nurse for their habitats back home (see Table 5.10).

Such an organised habitat will attract others such as banks and companies supplying agri-inputs and services to set up base in response to the opportunities in the rural hinterland. Thus, Navodaya Shahars will progressively grow into vibrant habitats that combine the best of urban services and expansive rural living.

The Bihar Land Reforms Commission (LRC) recommended allocation of land to 22.16 lakh landless households (16.68 lakh agriculture labourers and 5.48 lakh shelterless households of non-farm rural workers). The Navodaya Shahar model presented in this chapter works with these numbers and presents the implications of putting together, in various permutation and combination, the land distribution pattern recommended by LRC with the land units suggested by FAO (i.e., homegarden plots of 380 square metres).

The results of this exercise are interesting and encouraging. Take for example, Model NS-3 (in Table 6.2) which is built on the assumption that 5 lakh out of the 16.68 lakh agricultural labourer households are given plots as per the recommendation of LRC while the rest opt for plots of 380 square metre in Navodaya Shahars. The model further assumes that all the 5.48 lakh shelterless households of non-farm rural workers get plots in Navodaya Shahars—in this case, the unit recommended by LRC and FAO broadly coincide. After providing for 5 per cent extra land in Navodaya Shahars for infrastructure such as roads, public schools and hospitals, and an additional 25 per cent land for expansion of services, enterprises, commercial activities and for households from other economic classes, the total land requirement works out to be 6.09 lakh acres as against 13.9 lakh acres required for the implementation of the LRC recommendations.

At an average size of 5,000 households per Navodaya Shahar, nine such habitats will be required per district. Given such a network, the hinterland of each Navodaya Shahar will have a radius of 10 to 12 kms. This compact hinterland will enable households to progressively set foot into new opportunities while maintaining links with their traditional livelihoods and social network.

The size of each Navodaya Shahar works out to be around 610 acres. The cost of each plot will be Rs 20,000 to 30,000 which compares favourably with the subsidy provided in programmes such as IAY.

The proposed network of Navodaya Shahars will help Bihar compensate for the severe deficit that it suffers in terms of rural-urban linkages (see Table 6.1) while generating a massive programme for asset distribution and agricultural diversification at a manageable cost. The proposition is simple—unless Bihar creates such linkages at par with other states, it cannot aspire to reach or surpass their productivity and income levels.

Table 6.1

Districts and Class II-IV Towns in States

State	*Total No. of Districts*	*No. of Class II Towns*	*No. of Class III and IV Towns*
Andhra Pradesh	23	52	111
Bihar	38	19	92
Gujarat	26	36	179
Haryana	21	7	79
Karnataka	30	28	212
Kerala	14	24	125
Madhya Pradesh	50	26	343
Maharashtra	35	44	294
Orissa	30	15	114
Punjab	20	18	125
Rajasthan	33	27	176
Tamil Nadu	32	56	750
Uttar Pradesh	71	55	595
West Bengal	19	29	288

Source: The Census of India (2011), *Administrative Atlas of India* for data on districts across states and Kundu and Samanta (2011) for data on the number of towns in states.

The following sub-sections examine the evidence base on the benefits of the homegarden plots and the case for a new 'land reform plus' approach based on this modality.

Other sub-sections respond to many of the typical responses and queries that came up while presenting the Navodaya Shahar model to scholars and practitioners. What will be the impact of the diversion of land on agricultural output and food security? Can Navodaya Shahars be created given the current impasse on land acquisition? Why not develop the existing district towns and block headquarters instead of creating new habitats? Given that a large part of the citizens of Navodaya Shahars will be poor households, will these habitats be economically viable? Will Navodaya Shahars fit the social and cultural preferences of rural households? How is this model different from the traditional urbanisation approach? How is it different from PURA? These questions have deep significance for inclusive growth strategies.

6.2 Homegarden Plots: The Evidence based on Multiple Benefits

The role that homegarden plots are playing in economic terms and in the livelihoods of the masses is far more important than it is understood or acknowledged in the policy circles. In the Indian context, 'field research has shown that the provision of plots between 150-600 m^2 resulted in significant improvements in social status, annual income, increase in the borrowing capacity and in total family wealth' (Prosterman, 2010).

Based on an in-depth review of this modality across the globe, FAO and RDI studies highlight the following benefits from the homegarden plots (FAO):

i) Improved nutrition: Distribution of even relatively small amounts of land to land-poor families can provide a base for important improvements to the household nutrition. Some case studies show that small plots allowed households to consume more than the expert recommended allowance of vegetables (about twice the average), more fruits (about three times the normal consumption); and milk (about 60% more than average) (Prosterman, 2010).

In a study of Kerala wage earning families who cultivate homegarden plots occupying a fraction of an acre, Kumar (1978) found that the value of homegarden production was the most consistent positive predictor of child nutrition. It was a especially strong predictor of child nutrition during the slack employment season and in households in which the mother is not employed outside the home. Kumar concludes that given the strong correlation between homegardening and the presence of mothers not engaged in wage labour, distribution of land to landless and land-poor families may be a particularly fruitful strategy where employment opportunities for women are limited for societal or economic reasons. The very low work participation rates for females in rural Bihar matches with this scenario.

ii) Improvement in family's financial status: Homegardens generate livelihood benefits that go well beyond those related to nutrition and subsistence. In many cases, they generate cash incomes that allow the families to balance and enrich their overall consumption basket.

Box 6.1

Impact of Homegarden Plots on Family Income: Evidence Advanced by FAO

'It is a common misconception that homegardens are exclusively subsistence-oriented, whereas in fact homegardens provide households with cash crops as well as food crops (Hoogerbrugge and Fresco, 1993). In fact, returns to land and labour are often higher for homegardens than for field agriculture (Marsh, 1998). Homegardens can contribute to household income in several ways. The household may sell products produced in the homegarden, including fruits, vegetables, animal products and other valuable materials such as bamboo and wood for construction or fuel. The household may use the homegarden site to conduct cottage industries to produce crafts or small manufactures that can be sold (Marsh 1998).

The volume of homegarden production actually sold appears to be highly variable, with studies reporting that between 9 per cent and 51 per cent of production is sold (Hoogerbrugge and Fresco, 1993). Urban homegardens in Papua New Guinea are reported to have expanded over a period of several years (in one neighbourhood from a mean area of 125 m^2 in 1974 to a mean area of 817 m^2 in 1981), which the households attributed to opportunities to sell homegarden produce in local markets (Vasey, 1985). In the studied sample, 42.1 per cent of squatter households sold homegarden produce at the market, as compared to a district average of 25.8 per cent, indicating that the more impoverished households depended on homegardens more than the average (Vasey, 1985).

Livestock and tree crops produced on homegardens in southeastern Nigeria accounted for over 60 per cent of family cash income in one study (Okigbo, 1990). A study of urban and rural households in three Russian provinces found that two-thirds of all households obtained some income from agricultural home production, and in rural areas the market value of home production (computed using average local prices reduced by calculated market transaction costs) exceeds household labour income (tho Seeth *et al.*, 1998). In the Helen Keller International (HKI) pilot homegarden project in Bangladesh, 54 per cent of households reported selling homegarden products and earning the cash equivalent of 14.8 per cent of total average monthly income (HKI/AP, 2003).

contd...

...contd...

In addition to direct earnings from sale of homegarden production, production consumed by the household frees up household earnings for other purchases. In the Bangladesh HKI homegarden project, the income value of homegarden production increased from 14 per cent of average monthly income to 25 per cent after taking into account purchased fruits and vegetables (Marsh, 1998).

In some cases, a portion of the cash income from homegardens is used to purchase additional food for household consumption. A study of urban homegardens in the Philippines revealed that homegardening families spend less on food than non-gardening families, while homegardening families who plant a larger number of varieties of fruits and vegetables spend even less (Miura, 2003).

In Cambodia and Nepal, 31-65 per cent of income (31% in the case of Nepal and 65% in the case of Cambodia) derived from sale of poultry raised on homegardens was used to purchase other foods, while other proceeds were used to invest in production, education, savings and other purposes (HKI/AP, 2003). Urban homegardeners in Papua New Guinea sell various fruits at local markets and obtain cash that allows them to purchase rice that produces several times the food energy of the sold fruits (Vasey, 1985). Thus, homegardens provide households with a number of options by which they can satisfy their livelihood objectives, and each household can determine for itself what combination of consumption, trade and sale of homegarden production best fits its livelihood strategy.'

Source: Food and Agriculture Organisation of the United Nations (FAO). *Small Homegarden Plots and Sustainable Livelihoods for the Poor.* Economic and Social Development Department, FAO Corporate Document Repository. *http://www.fao.org/docrep/007/j2545e/j2545e01.htm# TopOfPage*

iii) Improved leverage in labour markets, enhanced social status and greater political participation: One objective to providing ownership to house and garden plots in some settings is to free agricultural labourers (or other wage labourers) from exploitive land-labour linkages. In the 1940's the Puerto Rican government distributed small homestead plots of between half an acre and one acre to the families of agricultural labourers. The idea behind the law was, in the words of Section 241 of the law, that it is a 'fundamental human right of all the human beings who live exclusively by the tilling of the soil, to be the owners of at least a piece.'

A survey of rural households in Karnataka, revealed that among households that had received small plots to construct homes and gardens, increased status within the village was the most cited benefit of ownership, surpassing even income and nutrition benefits; poorer households cited increased status even more often than other households (Hanstad *et al.*, 2002 cited in FAO).

In West Java, homegardens are an important symbol of social status, and households who are forced to build their house on homegardens owned by others are considered to be low status (Ahmad *et al.*, 1980, cited in Soemarwoto, 1987 and FAO). Increase in household status not only provide psychological benefits to household members, but are believed to provide households with better access to trade relations within the village, as well as better access to government programmes serving village households.

iv) Beneficial off-site environmental effects: Distribution of homegarden plots may also have beneficial off-site environmental effects. For example, where population pressures and lack of arable land threaten to push families to resettle in forests and wetlands, distribution of homegarden plots to landless and land-poor families can reduce pressures to migrate. This not only helps reduce conversion of lands better left as forests and wetland, but also allows families to remain in areas with established social services and markets for surpluses produced on the homegarden. In addition, distribution of homegardens may reduce the need for land-poor families to gather fodder and fuelwood from marginal lands, thereby contributing to the sustainability of such lands (FAO).

6.3 The 'Ideal' Size of Homegarden Plots

The realisation of benefits outlined above depends on the plot size. RDI's research in India indicates that the non-housing benefits of a homestead plot grow rapidly as the plot size increases beyond about 1,000 sq ft. The 'ideal' plot size for realisation of non-housing benefits ranges from 3,000 to 5,000 sq ft.

In a study of 62 rural homegardening households in Karnataka, researchers found that that there is a critical minimum plot size above which households begin planting more trees—the intensity of tree growing increased markedly once homegarden plot size reached 1,800 sq ft. The footprint of the house itself, which commonly occupies 500 sq ft or more of the plot, is presumed to reduce greatly the number of trees that can be planted on the smallest parcels (FAO).

Based on a sample survey of 97 land-poor households that had received house plots under government housing schemes in West Bengal, researchers found that the productive value of plots increased significantly with plot size until it reached approximately 3,000 sq ft (270 m^2) (Hansatd and Lokesh, 2002 cited in FAO). 'Homegardens smaller than 1,000 sq ft (90 m2) were found to provide the fewest benefits. Productive value and reported benefits increased significantly for homegardens of 1,000-1,999 sq ft (90-180 m^2), and increased further for homegardens of 2,000-2,999 sq ft (180-270 m^2), but then plateaued or even decreased for plots larger than 3,000 sq ft (270 m^2)' (Ibid.).

6.4 Possible Impact of Large Programmes for Creation of Homegarden Plots on the Availability of Arable Land, Overall Agricultural Productivity and Food Security

FAO concludes that even assuming that arable land is used to create homegardens, these risks are likely to be insubstantial for several reasons. First, because even very small plots can provide important benefits to families, the total amount of land needed for homegardens is likely to be modest. 'Assuming that 5 per cent of the acquired land is used to construct roads, drainage and other infrastructure, a one hectare plot could provide 380 square meter plots to 25 families. To place this in perspective, in India, distribution of 380 square meter plots to each of the nation's estimated 15 million completely landless families would require only 600,000 hectares of land, which is approximately 4/10 of 1 per cent of the nation's 161.8 million hectares of arable land' (FAO, also see Prosterman *et al.*, 2009).

Second, when homegarden plots are used to produce vegetables, fruits and animal products, they are likely to be yield at least as much agricultural value per unit area as had been generated on the arable land. 'A study of Javanese homegardens found that net income per square metre was higher for homegardens than for rice fields. The same study found that relative costs of production on home gardens were much lower than for rice fields (15.1% of gross income *versus* 55.9% of gross income for rice fields)' (Danoesastro, 1980 cited in Christanty, 1990 and FAO). The latter is particularly important for poor households, who typically have lower access to credit and are less capable of insuring against risk.

A study of well-developed homegardens in Karnataka concluded that homegarden plots could generate much higher income than is possible on commensurate arable land. 'The income per square meter is several multiples higher than on arable land in the same area used for grain crops' (Hanstad *et al.* cited in FAO). 'On a macro-scale, as indicated earlier, homegardens in Russia comprised about 4.5 per cent of total agricultural land in 2000, and yet were reported to have produced 64 per cent of all produce in the country, including 90 per cent of all potatoes and 75 per cent of fresh vegetables' (Borisova, 2000 cited in FAO).

Third, even if the output per hectare from the homegardens is less than on arable land, such effect is likely to be offset by the fact that homegardens directly service the need for food for a highly food-insecure segment of the population. This arrangement is likely to be much more efficient than other government food programmes. Moreover, families could decide better on the use of whatever is saved after self- consumption. (FAO).

6.5 Homegarden Plots: Implications in the Indian Context

In India, there has been some recognition of the potential benefits of homegarden plots. For example, the Tenth Plan noted that small plots amounting to a tenth of an acre (approximately 4,400 sq ft) and sometimes less, can provide the critical foundation of a diversified livelihood system, dramatically improve a rural family's nutrition, increase options for income-generation activities, create access to credit, and raise a household's status in a community. The Plan document concluded that small, well managed homestead plots could provide benefits unrealised by the decades of distributions of wasteland and ceiling surplus land (GoI, 2002).

The Central Government as well as a number of state governments, including the Government of Bihar have launched programmes in this area. But by and large, their scale and impact have been minimal because most of these programmes underestimate the livelihood potential of the home-garden plots and overestimate the costs—both the financial and the opportunity cost in terms of land use. Particularly, there is a widely held perception that homegarden plots are likely to reduce the amount of arable land, cause a fall in overall agricultural productivity and exacerbate food security concerns. As a result, this modality is used very sparingly to provide shelter to the homeless.

The guidelines on the homestead scheme' issued by the Ministry of Rural Development, Government of India (GoI MoRD, 2010) proves this point. These guidelines restrict the eligibility under the scheme to 'BPL households with neither land nor house-site.' Thus, large sections which have just a small home get excluded. Further, the above guidelines restrict the government assistance to purchase/acquisition of 100-250 square metres of land. This is much lower than the 'ideal' plot size for realisation of non-housing benefits.

Nielsen *et al.* (2006) points out, 'over the decades, the Government of India (GoI) and state governments have adopted a two-pronged approach to rural housing needs of the poor: (1) sites and services; and (2) house construction. Under the sites and services approach, the government provided sites (and in some cases) basic infrastructure facilities such as drinking water, roads, drainage, and community toilets for new layouts. The housing construction component has been largely targeted at those households that have already obtained house sites. Over the years, emphasis has shifted from sites and services to house construction. For example, almost 100 per cent of the GoI's flagship rural housing programme, IAY, is focused on construction of houses. Even when state governments do provide house sites, they are typically tiny—1,200 square feet or less—too small to capture the potential livelihood benefits associated with a 4,000 square foot plot. The homestead plot concept resurrects and revitalizes the original sites and services objective of rural housing programmes.'

Hanstad and Lokesh (2002) argues, 'in evaluating social value of distributing homegarden plots, it is useful to evaluate the efficacy of alternative programmes targeted to assist the same populations. In India, for example, we have found that government resources devoted to constructing housing for landless and land poor families might be better spent, and would reach more beneficiaries, if some portion of programme resources were diverted from housing construction and instead used to obtain larger house sites that provide space for home-gardening. Our own field research in India indicates that even the poorest rural households are able to accumulate the resources to construct a house (in stages) if they have secure rights to an adequate house site. For example in one study of 45 households who had received house sites from the government, 32 had constructed housing without government assistance, indicating that these families had the personal incentive, as well as access to sufficient materials or sufficient savings or access to credit to construct the house once they received land' (Hanstad and Lokesh, 2002 cited in FAO).

Overall, a highly minimalist approach to the homegarden plots modality has precluded the possibility of pitching it as an instrument to achieve some of the objectives behind blocked land reforms. This is a very big missed opportunity.

Nielson *et al.* (2006) concludes, 'land reform to broaden rural land access is still desperately needed in India. An estimated 17 million rural households are still completely landless and another 42 million households own less than 0.5 acre. The problems, however, will not be solved by relying solely on traditional land reform tools aiming to provide multiple acres for each land-poor household. Such goals are ideal, but often not feasible in the current political and fiscal environment. The central and state governments need to expand the number and type of tools in the land reform toolkit and prioritize improving land access for the most needy—those who have no land...providing landless households to landless households serves both objectives.'

The Navodaya Shahar model draws liberally on the excellent evidence base and analytics on homegarden plots generated by FAO and RDI, but goes far beyond it in the context of rural Bihar. This model argues for clustering of homegarden plots such that viable habitats are created to mount human development services, and progressively create a diversified livelihood base. As indicated earlier, the Navodaya Shahar model sees such clusters as a home-grown model to compensate for the clogged land reforms agenda on the one hand, and highly deficient rural-urban linkages and human development services in the vast rural expanse of the state on the other.

6.6 Comparing the Recommendations of the Bihar LRC and the Navodaya Shahar Model

The Bihar Land Reform Commission (LRC) recommended allotment of between 0.66 acre and 1.0 acre of ceiling surplus land to the lowest quintile of agricultural labourers consisting of 16.68 lakh households each and assignment of at least 10 decimals of land to shelterless households of 5.48 lakh non-farm rural workers each. This works out to a total land requirement of 13.89 lakh acres. However, this scale of land mobilisation was found to be difficult, and the LRC report has been put in cold storage.

Table 6.2 presents alternative scenarios for meeting the land distribution objective of LRC by bringing in the Navodaya Shahar model in progressive strength.

The size of each Navodaya Shahar is not large. Each Navodaya Shahar would be roughly the size of 3 square kilometres. If organised along the lines of linear towns in China, the need for local personal transport will be more or less eliminated.

In NS-3 Model, a total of 2.09 lakh acres will be required for 343 Navodaya Shahars. This works out to less than one per cent of Bihar's total land area. In NS-4 Model, a total of 2.49 lakh acres will be required as 50 per cent extra land is being provided. This works out to be 1.06 per cent of Bihar's total area. But the impact of this design could be dramatic.

Table 6.2

Alternative Scenarios for Meeting the Land Reform Objectives of Bihar LRC

Alternative Models	*16.68 lakh Agriculture Labourers*	*5.48 lakh Shelterless HHs of Non-Farm Rural Workers*	*Total Land Required for 22,16 lakh Landless HHs*	*Total Land Requ-ired for NS only*	*Total NS (NS per Dist-rict)@*	*Impact on Ratio of Urban+ Rur-ban (NS) Population/ Total Popu-lation@@*
LRC recomm-endation	Average of 0.8 acres to each of the 16.68 lakh agriculture labourer HHs	10 dec. or 0.1 acres to each HH	13.89 lakh acres	0	0	11.30%
NS-1*	10 lakh HHs given 0.8 acre each. Rest 6.68 lakh HHs given 380 sq mt plots in Navodaya Shahars	380 sq mt plot to each HH	9.48 lakh acres	1.48 lakh acres	243.2 (6.4)	28.30%
NS-2**	8.38 lakh HHs given 0.8 acre each. Rest 8.30 lakh HHs given 380 sq mt plots	380 sq mt plot to each HH	8.38 lakh acres	1.68 lakh acres	275.6 (7.25)	19.24%
NS-3***	5.00 lakh HHs given 0.8 acre each. Rest 11.68 lakh HHs given 380 sq mt plots	380 sq mt plot to each HH	6.09 lakh acres	2.09 lakh acres	343.2 (9.03)	21.90%
NS-4****	5.00 lakh HHs given 0.8 acre each. Rest 11.68 lakh HHs given 380 sq mt plots (assumption different from NS-3)	380 sq mt plot to each HH	6.49 lakh acres	2.49 lakh acres	343.2 (9.03)	21.90%

Note: NS-1*=Navodaya Shahar model 1. It is assumed that each Navodaya Shahar will host 5,000 HHs. Five per cent extra land is kept for infrastructure such as roads, schools and hospitals. In addition, 25 per cent extra land is provided for rural enterprise, commercial use and residents from other economic classes.

NS-2**= Navodaya Shahar model 2. The assumptions are same as above.

NS-3***= Navodaya Shahar model 3. The assumptions are same as above.

NS-4****= Navodaya Shahar model 4. Five per cent extra land is kept for infrastructure such as roads, schools and hospitals. In addition, 50 per cent extra land is provided for rural enterprise, commercial use and residents from other economic classes.

@= For NS1 to NS-3 Models, the size of each NS will be 610 acres. For NS-4 Model, the size of each NS will be 727 acres. This is because as compared to 30 per cent extra land (5 per cent for amenities plus 25 per cent for other uses) provided for in the former models, a total of 55 per cent extra land (5 per cent for amenities plus 50 per cent for other uses) is being allocated for in the latter (NS-4 Model).

@@= Assumes household size at six members per household. These percentages exclude the population that could be settled on the extra land provided in the above models. If these are added, the percentages estimates will be higher.

The last column in the above table attempts to highlight this. If Navodaya Shahars with quality amenities are considered as 'rur-ban habitats', there will be a dramatic change in the rural-urban structure in Bihar.

Thus, while the NS-3 model brings down the total land requirement to about half of the estimates of the Bihar LRC, its implications in terms of human development services and creation of livelihoods opportunities will be incomparable.

6.7 Can Navodaya Shahars be Created Given the Current Impasse on Land Acquisition?

The Navodaya Shahar model sees creation of these habitats as a highly profitable venture in the long run and envisages a public-private partnership (PPP) approach to create and share such gains. A farmers' association has succeeded in setting up a first class mini-township in Magarpatta in Pune. The same principle could be followed in creating Navodaya Shahars even though the target population here is not the upper middle class or the middle class.

The government needs to identify 2 to 3 alternative sites for each potential Navodaya Shahar. It should offer an attractive win-win package for people to respond to, and the area which offers land at the most attractive prices should be selected.

The package should comprise:

i) Offer to create a vibrant habitat by providing, to start with, a host of human development facilities. A certain minimum level will be through government's own resources. The rest will be by making land available to private entrepreneurs and supporting local entrepreneurs for such activities.

ii) Offer to buy 70 per cent of the land at the 'voluntary offer rate' (see below). The balance 30 per cent of the land should be returned as homegarden plots and/or space for enterprises, institutional and commercial use etc. This arrangement will ensure that all households contributing land retain a perpetual stake in the benefits to accrue from the development of the Navodaya Shahars.

iii) Landowners should have the freedom to choose the form in which they want back their 30 per cent share. The structure of the Navodaya Shahar (between homegarden plots and other uses) should be adjusted to such choices. However, dedicating three-fourths of the land retained to creation of homegarden plots will mean that the share of such plots in the overall land mass will not fall below 52.5 per cent.

iv) The owners should have the freedom to retain or sell such land freely after a moratorium of a reasonable period of 3 to 5 years. The moratorium is to prevent shortsighted or hasty decisions and not to prevent realisation of 'real estate gains'. If 'real estate gains' arise, they are an indicator of the success of the project, and flag the need for additional initiatives along these lines.

v) Some adjustment is required to the 30 per cent land return formula outlined above. Households who own and tender in less than 380 square metres should have the option of getting back one homegarden plot of 380 square metres or a commercial use plot of 150 square metres. At the other end too, for larger land parcels, say over three acres, the ratio of land to be returned would need to be moderated.

The discovery of the land price should be through the bids offered by the landowning households at alternative locations. The prospects of future gains from the 30 per cent land being returned, of good quality services and a host of new livelihood opportunities will induce people to offer attractive prices for the land being surrendered.

The government should develop suitable mechanisms to inspire confidence in the package that it offers. This market-based solution requires a market-based approach. The government's package (with regard to payment for land, return of land and for creating a minimum service level) should be backed by bank guarantees, so that the spectre of citizens not receiving full compensation for their assets even after three or four decades does not arise.

A cooperative structure should be created to manage the affairs of the Navodaya Shahar.

6.8 The Management Challenge

How will the state government manage the gigantic task of creating about 350 Navodaya Shahars?

First, the magnitude of this task in terms of land acquisition-related issues is less as compared to the recommendations of the Bihar LRC. This is because the quantum of land involved is smaller, but also because the nature of the land acquisition process is completely different. Here, peoples' resistance will be replaced by peoples' initiative. This is likely to make the task much more manageable and subject to much less litigation etc.

Second, dealing with 350 clusters rather than small pieces of land scattered all across the state will also make the task more manageable.

Third, the government's role is limited to developing and implementing the basic package and creating some basic services such as schools, hospitals and some arterial roads. Services such as electricity and water supply should be developed by other agencies in a PPP mode after reviewing the experience with PURA. Infact, there should be a conscious attempt to keep the role of the government to the minimum lest public funds are squandered in needless construction type activities. Such resources need to be conserved and directed to supporting poor households in acquiring homegarden plots and plots for other uses. The habitat should not be overbuilt at the start, but allowed to develop organically. The services should be allowed to grow in an entrepreneural mode.

As seen in Chapter 3, there are a number of programmes such as PMEGP which are not delivering any value. The financial and human resources involved in such programmes could be redeployed to this initiative.

Similarly, the major programme of REGP is grossly underperforming. In line with the new thrust on agriculture, REGP could be galvanised to create a host of agriculture-related infrastructure such as storage facilities in Navodaya Shahars.

Thus, if taken up with full political commitment, the Navodaya Shahar initiative will infact significantly enhance the delivery of public resources, and create a fountain of PPP and pure entrepreneurial efforts.

6.9 Will Navodaya Shahars be able to Create a Livelihood Base, in say 3 to 5 Years?

The above sub-sections throw light on the benefits generated by homegarden plots. Thus, landless households with plots in Navodaya Shahars are likely to gain a much stronger subsistence base. Those who owned equivalent plots elsewhere will also be better-off as an organised support structure in Navodaya Shahars is likely to improve the productivity of land and the price realisation for vegetables and fruits through more organised marketing, reduced wastage etc. Convergence with social security schemes is important. Making the new habitat eligible under Indira Awas Yojana and MNREGS will help the poorest in securing a plot and developing it.

Since Navodaya Shahars will not mean dislocation of more than 10 kms or so, the opportunities for wage income, sharecropping etc., availed by households earlier, will in all likelihood, continue to be accessible either through daily commutating or short-term local migration (say, of 3-4 days at a time).

Navodaya Shahars hold the promise of growing into habitats that the migrants have painted through their response to the question on 'changes needed at the origin' (see Table 5.10). The significant aggregate resource base (income, skill-base and enterprise) of the migrant population will be an important motive force for these habitats (see Box 5.2).

It is also important to keep in mind that the shift to the Navodaya Shahars will be gradual. For example, households who admit children into secondary schools in the new habitat may pitch-in a hut and only a part of the family may shift. As more remunerative wage, service or craft-related opportunities arise, the whole family may shift. It may sell its small piece of land in the village to make a *pucca* house in the new habitat or to establish a workshop. In other words, various kinds of transition strategies will be adopted by households depending on the changing relative livelihood and service prospects and needs. This is the usual process of mobility. Only, the Navodaya Shahar model is likely to make it more secure and easy.

On the other hand, the Navodaya Shahars will present a host of new opportunities. First, stepped up human development activities are likely to generate significant opportunities for wage labour and even regular salaried jobs. Second, construction activities and development of civic amenities as the Shahar stabilises and begins to attract the more well-off sections are likely to accelerate. These are highly labour intensive activities. Third, a range of service and production activities could be located based on the availability of local labour and the potential of the hinterland.

Take for instance, skill development activities. The previous chapter shows that unskilled labour dominates in the total migration flows from Bihar. Various studies highlight the need for upgradation of their skill base so that their earnings increase. Navodaya Shahars could thus evolve as skill development hubs. Singh (2010b) presents the basic architecture. It shows that providing skills to the masses could become the source of large scale entrepreneurial activities in the Navodaya Shahars. This will have a cascading effect across sectors (see Box 6.2).

Chapter 3 referred to a recent survey conducted by the Association for Social and Economic Transformation (ASET) which shows that around 33 per cent of total horticulture produce in Bihar goes waste. Navodaya Shahars with their abundant labour supply base could play an important role in creating a food processing base in backward districts. More broadly, Navodaya Shahars could evolve into a range of agri-related services that the Steering Group on Agriculture recommends and become an important institutional base for implementing the Government's new thrust on agriculture.

Similarly, banks and other service clusters linked to the rural hinterland are likely to set base progressively thereby further boosting employment and business opportunities. Locating some offices and residential quarters of public agencies will greatly help in augmenting the purchasing power in new settlements. Later on as the Navodaya Shahar matures, this will be dictated by its own merits—economic and programmatic.

To conclude, Navodaya Shahars are likely to erupt into a fountain of livelihood activities and much sooner than expected.

Box 6.2

Need for a New PPP-based Architecture for Skill Development of the Masses

The shortage of skills is preventing large segments of the population from being part of the India's growth story. The dismal performance hitherto however, suggests that the Eleventh Plan's ambitious vision needs a new architecture to reach the masses.

A solution emerges when we break the traditional mould of thinking with regard to PPP. India has created an impressive infrastructure in formal education and S&T. This infrastructure should be leveraged to create an organised back-end structure for generating high quality content for the skill development needs in the informal sector. Wide dispersal of such content could be ensured through micro-skill development academies which local entrepreneurs could set up in small towns, semi-urban areas and *bastis* and cater to potential demand in a convenient and cost-effective manner. A suitable franchise mechanism could ensure that these micro-skill development academies maintain requisite quality and financial viability.

The UNDP-supported project 'Skills and Knowledge for Improved Livelihoods and Living Standards' (SKILLS) bears out the promise of the above mechanisms in the context of the informal sector. The SKILLS project demonstrated that the PPP model it evolved is relevant not only for market-related skills, but also for skill sets involved in local livelihoods-support activities and self-employment in the informal sector.

The SKILLS project also demonstrated the power of ICT in bringing into the public space, the vast knowledge base across various skill trades that already exists but lies dormant or confined to apex promotional institutions such as KVIC. It further experimented with the use of ICT in creating mechanisms such as a web-based 'employment exchange' for informal sector workers on a highly localised and cost-effective basis.

However, the livelihood-linked needs and activities of small farmers, artisans and women's groups in the rural hinterland will require additional measures. For this stakeholder group, instead of one-time and fixed-duration group training, more flexible and longer-term handholding development support is required. The rural service enterprise model presented in the report 'Creating Vibrant Public-Private-Panchayat Partnership (PPPP) for Inclusive Growth' (Singh, 2010a) is relevant in this context. The Dungarpur case study in the report presents evidence to show that PPP-based rural service enterprise models that could ensure to each tribal family, an income of over Rs 25,000 per annum on 0.5 ha plots even in the context of a highly hostile eco-environment are feasible (see Box 3.1).

Source: Singh (2010b).

6.10 The Navodaya Shahar Model *versus* the Strategy of Developing/Improving Services in the Existing District Towns, Block Headquarters and Other Small Towns

The driving force of the Navodaya Shahar model is creation of assets for large number of poor households. This in turn opens up the possibility of creating human development services in a cost-effective manner. Will it be possible to achieve the former objective in the context of the existing district towns, block headquarters and other small towns?

Contrary to the popular perception, land prices in district and block headquarters and even in small urban-type habitats are quite high. For example, a one *kattha* plot (equivalent to 1,365 sq ft) in a small road-side hamlet on the Katihar-Purnia highway commands the price of Rs 15 to 20 lakh. Such high prices prevail even in backward districts because of the huge premium that a urban-type habitat with access to infrastructure such as roads and electricity begins to command. A couple of kilometres into the interior, the land prices drop considerably.

Such high land prices in existing urban habitats will preclude accommodation of the poor in large numbers, or for that matter, even in small numbers in dignified living.

But by and large, development of district and block headquarters and creation of Navodaya Shahars are seen as complimentary and not competing processes. The quality and vibrancy of Navodaya Shahars will depend on the dynamism that the district/block headquarters are able to display. The Navodaya Shahars in turn, are likely to contribute to such vibrancy. For example, improvement in dropout rates at the secondary education level will increase the demand for college seats in the district capital. This will be true for health services too. Similarly, an increase in output and purchasing power at the lower tiers will enhance economic and commercial activities at the district/block headquarters level.

Thus, the relevant question for the district and block level urban habitats is: How will they make effective use of the increased demand for services that is likely to emerge from the chain of Navodaya Shahars?

6.11 Likely Impact of Navodaya Shahars on Services across Rural Areas

Given budgetary constraint, will services in Navodaya Shahars be at the cost of their wider dispersal across rural areas? Will it ease the pressure for universalistion of services in interior areas?

Performance data on programmes dealing with social services and rural infrastructure shows that utilisation rates are woefully low. Thus outlays for human development services and infrastructure in Navodaya Shahars are not likely to make a dent into fund availability for other areas. On the contrary, Navodaya Shahars are likely to impact the facilities in surrounding areas in a positive manner. First, one of the main causes for poor services in deep rural hinterland is high absenteeism of personnel. Teachers and health workers from outside the district are reluctant to set homes in rural areas. Navodaya Shahars are likely to encourage such personnel to set homes there.

Lack of public pressure for improved services is another important cause for their poor standards in rural areas. Thus, improved standards in Navodaya Shahars are likely to create a positive demonstration effect.

Most important, a complimentarity is envisaged between the needs of the countryside and the facilities that are created at Navodaya Shahars. For example, availability of secondary schools at Navodaya Shahars along with suitable accommodations for families is likely to encourage students in the hinterland to continue education at the middle school level. Thus, the dropout rates may come down.

There has been a spurt in private activities in the education and health sectors. Particularly, they have created a good clientele amongst the migrant labour families who have some cash income. Navodaya Shahars may provide an opportunity to expand and grow these initiatives in an orderly fashion. This will be of immense value to the entire hinterland.

6.12 The Navodaya Shahar Model *versus* the Traditional Urbanisation Approach

How is the Navodaya Shahar model different from the traditional urbanisation approach?

Traditional urbanisation is led by the rich, wealthy and resourceful. Poor households mostly seek low paid, casual and informal work in such habitats. Often their living conditions and human development baseline are worse than in rural areas.

On the other hand, the starting point in the Navodaya Shahar model is creation of secure and productive assets for the poor as well as access to human development services. The livelihood opportunities emerge out of this asset ownership and removal of the lid from their own huge backlog in human development attainment. As such, under the Navodaya Shahar model, the poor households are no longer the low cost service providers to others but constitute the mainstream which collectively lifts itself out of poverty.

Thus, seen from the point of view of the poor, the Navodaya Shahar model is an antithesis of the traditional urbanisation process. But its returns are similar to a traditional urbanisation process.

6.13 The Navodaya Shahar Model *versus* the Government of India's Flagship PURA Initiative

The Ministry of Rural Development (MoRD), Government of India has relaunched the scheme, Provision of Urban Amenities in Rural Areas (PURA)' as a Central sector scheme during the remaining period of the Eleventh Plan. This has been done through technical assistance from ADB.

The scheme seeks to deliver a basket of infrastructure and amenities in the rural areas and harness private sector efficiencies in the management of assets and delivery of services. PURA is seen as a catalyst not only for convergence between different infrastructure development schemes but also for a new model for the management of urbanisation of rural areas.

The package of services include: roads, water supply and sewerage, drainage, solid waste management, streetlighting and power distribution. Private players selected through open bidding are expected to create such assets and maintain it for 10 years. There is an expectation that the private player will add on some revenue-earning economic activities such as village linked tourism, integrated rural hub, rural market, agri-common services centre, warehousing, skill development etc. PURA projects are to be taken in a *gram panchayat* or a cluster of geographically contiguous *gram panchayats* with a population of about 25,000-40,000.

During this pilot phase, the cost of each PURA project shall be limited to a maximum of Rs 120 crore. The capital grant is limited to a maximum of 35 per cent of the project cost. This is to be funded from a Plan outlay of Rs 248 crore.

The eligibility criteria for the private sector entities include a minimum net worth of Rs 25 crore and experience of developing infrastructure projects having a cumulative value of at least Rs 50 crore. (GoI).

While both PURA and the Navodaya Shahar model aim to enrich amenities in rural areas, their underlying strategies are quite distinct.

First, while PURA focusses on providing amenities of urban standards in rural areas, the main objective of the Navodaya Shahar model is to create an asset base for the assetless.

Second, PURA focusses on services such as water supply and sewerage, roads, drainage, solid waste management, streetlighting and power distribution. While PURA guidelines also envisage some economic and skill development activities, these seem like an 'add-on.' On the other hand, the Navodaya Shahar model accords priority to human development infrastructure such as schools and health centres. While electricity and arterial roads are important for any habitat, the Navodaya Shahar model seeks to consciously de-emphasise costly solutions in other areas. It seeks to conserve resources for creating assets for the poor.

Third, the 2001 Census observed that 61.6 per cent of the migrant population moves within a district. Thus, the Navodaya Shahar model is designed to support a degree of mobility that strengthens the triple bottom line of the *aam admi*. This is diametrically opposite to PURA which is designed to curb mobility.

A look at the project's financial norms drives homes the impracticality of PURA in the context of backward disticts with their predominantly rural population and severe infrastructure defeciencies. This is the position in respect of a majority of the districts in Bihar.

Further, PURA prescribes implementation by large contractors with a minimum net worth of Rs 25 crore. The *panchayats* have virtually no role to play. The Navodaya Shahar on the other hand envisages burgeoning of local enterprise.

An evaluation of PURA pilot projects in seven locations by National Institute of Rural Development (NIRD) found that convergence with ongoing schemes was missing. The report suggested taking up PURA around fast growing industrial area/towns. It further suggested that rather than mere creation of connectivity, PURA should also focus on livelihoods in rural areas and spur efforts to improve linkages for production in all productive sectors including industries. Thus, while PURA may be suitable for clusters that have already reached or have the potential to reach a threshold density of economic activity and population, it is not relevant for scenarios that prevail in the 150 backward districts in the country.

7 Conclusions and Policy Implications

7.1 Introduction

In Bihar, a number of powerful factors intersect to create a vortex of multidimensional poverty. These include near total assetlessness in more than half of the rural population, highly suboptimal baseline in terms of human development, deep social stratification and gender divide. On top of it is the prospect of stagnation in the rural-urban ratio at the astonishingly low level of around 10 to 12 per cent as projected by the Expert Group on Population.

The above structural configuration severely restricts the policy choices in the medium term. This is clear from the results over the first five-year term of the NDA government. The spectacular growth rate post-2005 was led by a release of pent up consumption demand and recovery in governmental spending which contributes nearly a fourth of Bihar's GSDP. By concentrating all resources in almost a campaign mode, the state government was able to transform areas such as primary education and immunisation. But indicators that are reflective of deeper structural characteristics refuse to budge. For example, at the secondary and senior secondary levels, the dropout rates continue to be as high as 80 to 90 per cent. Indicators of antenatal care and reproductive health in rural areas remain sluggish. The growth rates in the agriculture sector continue to swing wildly from year to year. The credit deposit ratio shows sluggishness at a dismal level of around 32 per cent. The inter-district disparities in almost all indicators are very sharp.

It is clear that Bihar will have to carve out its own model of inclusive development. Particularly, the state government will have to evolve innovations to derive benefits normally associated with urban transformation, out of a predominantly rural baseline. But this is not a matter of providing urban amenities in the existing rural habitats as programmes such as PURA seem to suggest—forget the cost of creating such amenities, their upkeep itself will be infeasible. The development challenge calls for a coordinated effort at addressing the triple bottom line of the poor households in rural areas.

The strategic components of such an approach include emphasis on asset creation for the masses and upgrading of the group approach to that of habitat-level convergence. This is necessary for triggering a virtuous cycle of livelihood generation from the unmet human development needs. Safe and secure mobility for the most vulnerable households is another pillar. These strategic elements are organically related and must be configured accordingly.

This is the 'land reform plus' agenda that forms the base of the Navodaya Shahar model outlined in this book.

The Government of Bihar will have to pick up individual national programmes with their disparate orientation and reconfigure them into a cohesive framework on the above lines. Individual strands need to come together to trigger a virtuous cycle that starts with subsistence security based on access to assets and human development services and matures to stable income and wealth generation. But this is going to be a daunting challenge requiring a fundamental realignment in the state government's own policies, programmes, machinery and processes. Dismal performance in programmes such as RIDF shows that the state government is yet to evolve an integrated vision of rural infrastructure and needs to chart a new course.

In the context outlined above, the following sub-sections analyse the relevance of some of the major contemporary policy initiatives and programmes at the Central and state level, and explore the possible direction for their realignment.

7.2 Evolving a 'Land Reform Plus' Agenda based on LRC Recommendations and the Roadmap for Agriculture: The Navodaya Shahar Model

Soon upon assuming power in 2005, the NDA government decided to revive the initiative in land reforms. This was a step in the right direction.

Thus, even if the modalities suggested by LRC are found to be socially and politically difficult, the LRC's main message should not be lost track of.

The Steering Group on Vision of Agriculture Development in Bihar (2010) suggests some important strategies to move forward. Its recommendation for market-based mechanisms for securing land to small and marginal farmers could be extended to 'supplement' the objective of securing land to the landless.

But there is a need to go much further than the road map suggested by the Steering Group. It is important to realise that given the size of the population dependant on agriculture and the underlying structural characteristics, development in this vast domain in a medium-term perspective is not a sectoral agenda. The desired breakthrough will not materialise unless policy and programmatic initiatives in agriculture set into motion a broader rural reorganisation process. Such reorganisation must encompass asset creation for the poor on the one hand, and upgrading the baseline in terms of human development services as well as a whole range of community services and enterprises on the other.

Normally this broader change agenda is carried on the wings of rural-urban transformation. But the demographic structure in Bihar has already reached a configuration that renders it incapable of emerging out of the huge backlog. Thus, this transformation will have to be carried forward through a carefully designed programme of 'land reform plus'. Chapter 6 on the Navodaya Shahar model presents the implications of this approach.

The Navodaya Shahar model is built on the premise that reduction in the plot size to be allocated to landless households due to the pressure on land and/or social complexities can be made up by clustering such plots to create a host of other benefits such as human development services. The evidence advanced by FAO based on its global research suggests that home and garden plots of 380 square metres can provide a certain livelihood base to poor households, and need to be considered seriously as a feasible land reform option in scenarios of extreme distress in land availability.

Table 6.2 (Chapter 6) shows the dramatic implications of this new approach. By introducing it into the calculus of providing land to 22.16 lakh families as suggested by LRC, a network of around 350 habitats (Navodaya Shahars) or nine per districts can be created. Each habitat will have an average size of 5,000 households and occupy a compact area of about 3 square kilometres. These habitats will together consume less than one per cent of Bihar's total area, but create a network of organised 'rur-ban' habitats whose total population size will be equal to the total existing urban population in Bihar. Thus, while these models would bring down the land requirement *vis-à-vis* the estimates of the Bihar LRC, their implications in terms of human development services and creation of livelihoods opportunities will be incomparable.

Ownership of assets by the poor households and feasible solutions for services will provide a solid base for livelihood and democracy. Political commitment could transform the Navodaya Shahars or Navodaya Grams into the 21st century incarnation of Mahatma Gandhi's Gram Swaraj vision.

7.3 Public-Private-Community Partnership (PPCP)

How will such a complex task be achieved? The answer is that what looks to be quite a complex process is actually organic in nature. Once structural roadblocks are removed, the process will gather momentum on its own.

In any case, given the extent of the development deficit in Bihar, it is clear that public resources and machinery will not suffice to meet the challenge. Thus, Bihar needs a solid framework for PPCP to address its vast development challenges. Chapter 6 outlines a PPP framework for the creation of Navodaya Shahars. The creation of a suitable network of habitats of certain size and quality will give a further fillip to PPP and private enterprise across sectors. It is not incidental that the banking infrastructure in rural Bihar is weak.

The transaction costs of PPP/PPCP need to be brought down. But they remain enormously high not only because of weak physical infrastructure. First, the basic vision is weak as shown by the low utilisation rates in the Rural Infrastructure Development Fund (RIDF). Second, restrictive rules combined with large grey areas where taking any partnership initiative requires long, cumbersome and costly efforts at breaking new grounds also contribute to the problem. As a result, poorer areas and sections of the population continue to remain unserved by the wider economic forces and institutions. Thus, public policy support to PPCP/PPP needs to move away from incremental or partial measures such as allocation of some resources for subsiding such initiatives to addressing the core issues and institutional bottlenecks responsible for the enormously high transaction costs (Singh, 2010a). The Navodaya Shahar model could provide the framework for a broad-based PPCP initiative.

The most vital link in the PPCP chain is the strengthening of community capacity. This includes issues such as property rights for the poor, both for the assets held individually and for community resources. The Navodaya Shahar model will be successful only if masses are able to reorganise their small landholdings and homesteads through a regime of secure property rights for the poor.

7.4 Leveraging National Programmes

The Swarnjayanti Gram Swarozagar Yojana (SGSY) and the National Rural Livelihood Mission (NRLM)

SGSY, the flagship anti-poverty programme of the Government of India since 1999 focusses on creating self-employment by organising the poor into self-help groups (SHGs). Its new incarnation, the National Rural Livelihood Mission (NRLM) essentially continues with the basic SGSY approach, but seeks to build an elaborate institutional support structure from the national level to the sub-district level. NRLM aims to strengthen the social mobilisation process and expand the mechanisms for loans, subsidies, capital grants, skill development support, technical support etc., for the activities of SHGs and their federations.

In the structural configuration of Bihar, however, promoting small group-based income generation activities while useful in some areas, may largely be like filling a bucket with large holes. There is a need to lift the baseline itself through convergent action. In the specific context of Bihar where poverty is deep and dense, the 'triple bottom line' approach with asset creation for the masses as an entry point appears to be more relevant than both the income-generating approach and the service delivery approach.

Social capital building through SHGs is at the core of NRLM. This is important. But the Navodaya Shahar model seeks to take it to the level of a habitat, as such an approach is expected to broaden the developmental scope to create a cycle of asset creation, generation of services and livelihood opportunities.

NRLM guidelines talk of forging convergence with other relevant programmes of the government. In reality, this hardly ever materialises across programmes formulated with their separate mandates and operational procedures. On the other hand, synergy amongst individual elements is at the very core of the triple bottom line approach and the Navodaya Shahar model. Thus for example, provision of services (including agri-extension services) and other opportunities for income generation would reduce the size of land parcels that need to be distributed. This would make land reforms more practicable. Similarly, creation of habitats of a certain size would help in organising services. Such an organically convergent approach would help generate a dynamic livelihood cycle.

The Navodaya Shahar model also has the advantage of internalising mobility as a strategy for generating a combined cycle of asset creation, subsistence security, human development, and income generation.

The guidelines for NRLM available on the website of the Union Ministry of Rural Development emphasise a demand-driven strategy. They clarify, 'states will have the flexibility to develop their action plans for poverty reduction which will include a 7 year Perspective Plan and a detailed Annual Action Plan. The overall plan will be within the allocation for the state based on inter-se poverty ratios...' (GoI, 2011d).

The Government of Bihar needs to avail of this scope for flexibility and tailor NRLM to the proposed 'land reform plus' agenda and the Navodaya Shahar model. This exercise should include 'Jeevika' which is the World Bank-supported State Livelihoods Mission. Similarly, programmes such as RIDF need to be integrated in this framework. Thinly spread programmes for delivery of services (e.g. PMEGP) and for social security, each working in isolation, also need to be similarly reprogrammed.

Cash Subsidies

In his budget speech in March 2011, the Union Finance Minister proposed direct cash subsidy to the poor. This idea has been received well, even though some doubts persist as to its workability on the ground. While some of the best minds in India work on the rather formidable design challenges, it is an opportune moment to explore its implications in relation to the Navodaya Shahar model.

The popularity of cash transfers to the poor is based on the positive social spin-offs of the 'conditional' cash transfer programmes in some South American countries. The most prominent amongst these is *Bolsa Família* in Brazil. This monthly cash transfer is provided to poor families on conditions of school attendance by children and adolescents, and responsiveness to the basic health care of young children, expectant women and lactating mothers. It reaches more than 46 million people thereby covering a large proportion of the country's low-income population. However, the UNDP study conducted by Barrows *et al.* (2009) shows that the recent decline in inequality and consequent poverty reduction in Brazil are the result of three main forces working together: (a) an increase in contributory and non-contributory government transfers, (b) a decline in wage differentials by educational level and reductions in the inequality in education caused by an accelerated expansion of labour force educational level, and (c) an improvement in spatial and sectoral integration of labour markets resulting in a movement of Brazil's economic activity towards non-metropolitan areas.

In the baseline of Bihar, cash subsidies will reach their transformational potential only if they are combined with a strong programme of asset creation for the poor. Cash transfers in an organised manner could play a truly transformational role in the context of the Navodaya Shahar model by hedging the risks for poor households in their mobility towards a new regime crafted to enrich their asset base and progressively their 'triple bottom line'.

7.5 Policy on Migration

Chapter 5 brought out the importance of migration in the livelihood of the households in rural Bihar.

Chapter 5 shows that migration may be affecting about one-third to one-half of the rural households in Bihar. Some studies showed that two out of three people who belonged to the economically active age group (14-44 years) migrated.

The proportion of migrant households receiving remittances is very high. An IIPA study indicates that it may be as high as 99 per cent. This study concludes that, the average figure of Rs 15,622 turns to be extremely significant as it almost wipes out the deficit that the average migrant family faces on account of the mismatch between its expenditure and income from land and cattle. A study by IHD, estimated that remittance constituted 47.2 per cent of the total family income. The IIPA study estimates the total value of remittances to be Rs 7,500 crore in a year. According to this study, 'the amount is more than the state government's own revenue and about 4-5 times the state's annual plan expenditure. For the poor households, the amount is invaluable as the average remittance (per household) is slightly higher than the state's per capita income.' But very little of this resource goes into strengthening the asset base of the migrant households.

The migration rates seem to have levelled off. Perhaps, this is a temporary phenomenon due to NREGA and the recent spurt in economic activity. But given the medium-term projection of the Expert Group on Population Projection, it is quite clear that the growing population of Bihar in the midst of frozen rural-urban ratios will continue to migrate out in large volumes. Thus, the state needs to develop a policy that supports the migrants both at the point of destination and at the point of origin.

A number of studies have outlined measures in this regard. These include: creation of suitable identity devices, a tracking and complaint registration system, skill development so that their earning potential increases, secure mechanisms for money transfer, increasing awareness about vulnerabilities such as HIV/AIDS etc.

This study flags the need for a policy to facilitate productive use of their hard earned resources at the origin. Table 5.10 (Chapter 5) which presents their expectations with regard to conditions required at the point of origin shows that the gap between the expectation and reality is yawning. The Navodaya Shahar model should be seen in this light. Such habitats will provide an opportunity to the migrant population to start accumulating assets systematically and create a niche that they could return to once their basic economic objectives have been met. Conversely, the migrant population, their income, skill base and enterprise will be an important source for maturation of the Navodaya Shahars.

The IHD study indicates that two-thirds of the origin households wanted the migrants to return to the village and a similar percentage of the migrants expressed desire to ultimately settle down in their origin village. Many migrants indicated that if some industries or other income generating activities are established in their village they would willingly go back as Delhi was fast becoming a costly city, making migration economically non-viable. Such dreams cannot be compromised.

7.6 Towards an Integrated Bihar Nav-Nirman Programme

The change from a service delivery-driven approach to the "triple bottom line" approach will require a major transformation in the existing administrative structure and development management system which have mounted incredible human misery.

First, the major rural-urban fault line within the government needs to be bridged. Policy circles need to wake up to the reality that the rigid bifurcation of government functioning into 'rural development' and 'urban development' strands seems to be creating a roadblock in what is meant to be a natural and seamless process in the business of societies and the lives of the *aam admi*. This schism is also stunting the decentralisation process which is meant to converge the urban and rural strands on the ground in a locally relevant and empowered framework.

There is a need for bold and original thinking lest initiatives such as Navodaya Shahars meet the fate of stillborn in the turf war between the Rural Development Department and the Urban Development Department, and similar bifurcation within other departments. There is need for a new organising principle—the Bihar Nav-Nirman Programme to galvanise all resources for a joint attack on the spectre of mass multidimensional poverty.

The Navodaya Shahar model presents a suitable starting point for conceptualising and launching the Bihar Nav-Nirman Programme.

There is no escape from development re-engineering of a fundamental nature. Since between 2010 and 2030, UP, Bihar and MP will account for 40 per cent of the increase in the 15-59 year bracket in the country, conventional development models are likely to convert this 'potential demographic dividend' into a nightmare.

Such development re-engineering will require strong political leadership as well as a massive administrative effort. At the current juncture, the Chief Minister, Nitish Kumar is well endowed in both these arenas and uniquely placed to take this giant leap in inclusive development.

References

Alkire, Sabina and Maria Emma Santos (2010). *Acute Multidimensional Poverty: A New Index for Developing Countries.* Oxford Poverty and Human Development Initiative. *http://www.ophi.org.uk/acute-multidimensional-poverty-a-new-index-for-developing-countries/*

ASI Report (2007-08). *Annual Survey of Industries.* Ministry of Statistics and Programme Implementation.

Asian Development Bank (2008). "India: Preparing the Bihar Urban Development Project", *Technical Assistance Report 41603*, July.

Bandyopadhyay, D. (2009). "Lost Opportunity in Bihar", *Economic & Political Weekly* XLIV(47), November 21.

Bardhan, Pranab (2010). "Awakening Giants: Feet of Clay", Princeton NJ: Princeton University Press.

Barrows, Ricardo, Mirela de Carvalho and Sameul Franco (2009). *Markets, the State and the Dynamics of Inequality: The Case of Brazil.* UNDP. *http://economiccluster-lac.org/images/pdf/desarrollos-Incluyentes/14_RPPLAC_ID.pdfc*

Bhaskaran, Resmi P. and Balwant Singh Mehta (2010). *Tracing Migrants in Delhi from Bihar: An Enquiry on the Role of Migration as a Development Facilitator in Poor Origin Areas.* New Delhi: Institute of Human Development.

Bihar Rural Livelihoods Promotion Society (2007). "Poverty and Social Assessment: A District-wise Study of Bihar", *Jeevika.* Project Implementation Plan. Government of Bihar. *http://www.brlp.in/admin/Files/Poverty%20and%20Social% 20Assessment%20A%20districtwise%20study%20of%20B.pdf*

Borisova, Y. (2000). "Land Ownership Remains Russian Privatisation's Final Frontier", *The St. Petersburg Times (Russia).*

Census (2011). *Provisional Population Totals, Paper 1 of 2011 India Series 1*, Chapter-6 (State of Literacy). Office of the Registrar General and Census Commissioner of India, Ministry of Home, Government of India

Christanty, L. (1990). "Home Gardens in Tropical Asia, with Special Reference to Indonesia", in K. Landauer and M. Brazil (eds.), *Tropical Home Gardens.* Tokyo, Japan: United Nations University Press.

CLEP and UNDP (2008). "Making the Law Work for Everyone", *Report of the Commission on Legal Empowerment of the Poor.* Volume 1. New Jersey: Toppan Printing Company America Inc.

Danoesastro, H. (1980). "The Role of the Home Garden as a Ssource of Additional Family Income", *Seminar on the Ecology of Homegardens, III.* Bandung, Indonesia: Institute of Ecology.

Datt, Gaurav and Martin Ravallion (2010). "Shining for the Poor Too?", *Economic & Political Weekly* XLV(7), February 13.

Deshingkar, Priya, Sushil Kumar, Harendra Kumar Chobey and Dhananjay Kumar (2006). *The Role of Migration and Remittances in Promoting Livelihoods in Bihar*. London: The Overseas Development Institute. December.

Ekta Parishad and Praxis (2009). *Landlessness and Social Justice: An Assessment of Disparities in Land Distribution and Prospects of Land Reforms.* Patna.

Equity Foundation (2011). *Economic Participation of Women in Bihar.* Socio-Economic Research Division, Planning Commission. *http://planningcommission.nic.in/reports/sereport/ser/ser_women.pdf*

Food and Agriculture Organisation of the United Nations FAO (2002). *Production Yearbook*.

——. (n.d.). *Small Homegarden Plots and Sustainable Livelihoods for the Poor.* Economic and Social Development Department, FAO Corporate Document Repository. *http://www.fao.org/docrep/007/j2545e/j2545e01.htm#TopOfPage*

GoB (2010). *Towards Accelerated Agricultural Development in Bihar,* Steering Group on Vision of Agriculture Development in Bihar. Department of Agriculture, Government of Bihar.

——. (2011). *"Bihar Economic Survey 2010-11*. Government of Bihar. *http://gov.bih.nic.in/documents/Economic-Survey-2011-English.pdf*

GoI (2011a). *Economic Survey 2010-11.* New Delhi: Ministry of Finance. *http://indiabudget.nic.in/survey.asp*

——. (2011b). *Provisional Population Totals Paper 1 of 2011 India Series 1*. New Delhi: Office of the Registrar General & Census Commissioner India.

——. (2011c). *Guidelines on PURA.* New Delhi: Ministry of Rural Development. *http://rural.nic.in/PURA/PURA%20Scheme%20Guidelines.pdf*

——. (2011d). *National Rural Livelihood Mission: Framework for Implementation.* New Delhi: Ministry of Rural Development. *http://rural.nic.in/latest/NRLM_lattest_13092010.pdf*

——. (2011e). *Guidelines of the Homestead Scheme.* New Delhi: Ministry of Rural Development. *http://rural.nic.in/Presentation/IAY_PPT_05052010.pdf*

——. (2010). *Guidelines of the Homestead Scheme.* Ministry of Rural Development. *http://rural.nic.in/Presentation/IAY_PPT_05052010.pdf*

——. (2009). *India Urban Poverty Report, 2009.* Ministry of Urban Development. Oxford University Press.

——. (2008). *Eleventh Five Year Plan* (2007-12). Planning Commission of India.

——. (2006). "Population Projections for India and States 2001-2026", *Report of the Technical Group on Population Projections.* Constituted by the National Commission on Population, (May). New Delhi: Office of the Registrar General & Census Commission.

——. (2002). *Tenth Five-Year Plan*. New Delhi: Planning Commission of India.

Hanstad, T. and S.B. Lokesh (2002). "Allocating Homestead Plots as Land Reform: Analysis from West Bengal", *RDI Report on Foreign Aid and Development* 115: 10-11. Rural Development Institute.

Hanstad, Tim, J. Brown and R. Prosterman (2002). "Larger Homestead Plots as Land Reform?: International Experience and Analysis from Karnataka", *Economic & Political Weekly* 37(29): 3053-62.

Hanstad, Tim, Robin Nielsen and Jennifer Brown (2004). *Land and Livelihoods: Making Land Rights Real for India's Rural Poor*. FAO. May.

Hanstad, Tim, S.B. Lokesh and M. Asum (2003). *Reaping the Rewards of Homestead Gardens: Nutritional and Income Benefits from Homestead Plots in Karnataka'*. FAO.

Hanstad T., T. Haque and R. Nielsen (2008). "Improving Land Access for India's Rural Poor, *Economic and Political Weekly* 3: 49-55.

Helen Keller International/Asia-Pacific (2003). *Integration of Animal Husbandry into Home Gardening Programmes to Increase Vitamin A Intake from Foods: Bangladesh, Cambodia and Nepal. http://hkiasiapacific.org/_downloads/APO percent20Special percent20issue percent20Jan percent202003.pdf)*

Himanshu, Peter Lanjouw, Abhiroop Mukhopadhyay and Rinku Murgai (2011). "Non-Farm Diversification and Rural Poverty Decline: A Perspective from Indian Sample Survey and Village Study Data", *Asia Research Centre Working Paper* 44, London School of Economics & Political Science, Asia Research Centre.

Hoogerbrugge, I. and Fresco, L.O. (1993). "Homegarden Systems: Agricultural Characteristics and Challenges", *Gatekeeper Series* No. 39. International Institute for Environment and Development.

IFAD (2011). *Rural Poverty Report.* Italy: IFAD.

Institute of Human Development (2010). *International Seminar on Poverty in Bihar: Patterns, Dimensions and Eradication Strategies.* Patna. April 18-20. *http://www.ihdindia.org/pdf/Poverty_Seminar_Report.pdf*

Krishna and Vajpai (2011). "Lineal Spread and Radial Dissipation: Experiencing Growth in Rural India, 1993-2005", *Economic & Political Weekly* XLVI(38): 44-51, September 17.

Kundu, Debolina and Dibiyendu Samanta (2011). "Redefining the Inclusive Urban Agenda in India", *Economic & Political Weekly* XLVI(5): 55-63, January 29.

Kumar, Girish and Pranab Banerji (2010). *A Study of Bihari Migrant Labourers: Incidence, Causes and Remedies*. The Indian Institute of Public Administration (IIPA).

Kumar, S.K. (1978). "Role of the Household Economy in Child Nutrition at Low Incomes: A Case Study in Kerala", *Occasional Paper* No. 95. Department of Agricultural Economics, Cornell University pp.60-61.

Lanjouw, Peter and Rinku Murgai (2009). "Poverty Decline, Agricultural Wages and Nonfarm Employment in Rural India: 1983-2004", *Agricultural Economics* 40(2): 243-263, March.

LRC (2007). *Interim Report on Some Issues Relating to Bhoodan in Bihar*, Bihar Land Reforms Commission.

Mainstream (2009). *Mainstream* XLVII(33), August 1.

Marsh, R. (1998). "Building on Traditional Gardening to Improve Household Food Security", *Food, Nutrition and Agriculture* No. 22. Food and Agriculture Organization.

Mitchell, Robert and Tim Hanstad (2004). *Small Homegarden Plots and Sustainable Livelihoods for the Poor*. FAO. *(ftp://ftp.fao.org/docrep/fao/007/j2545e/j2545e00.pdf)*

Miura, S., K. Osamu and W. Susumu (2003). "Home Gardening in Urban Poor Communities of the Philippines", *International Journal of Food Sciences and Nutrition* 54(1).

Nielsen R., T. Hanstad and L. Rolfes/Rural Development Institute (RDI) (2006). "Implementing Homestead Plot Programmes Experience from India," *LSP Working Paper* 23. Food and Agriculture Organisation of the United Nations, Livelihood Support Programme (LSP).

NSSO (2009), "Housing Condition and Amenities in India", *Report 535, NSS 65th Round (July 2007-June 2008)*. Ministry of Statistics and Programme Implementation, Government of India. Nevember.

———. (2010a). "Household Consumer Expenditure in India", *NSSO Report 530, 64th Round (July 2007-June 2008)*. Ministry of Statistics and Programme Implementation, Government of India. March.

———. (2010b). "Employment and Unemployment Situation in India", *NSSO Report 531, 64th Round (July 2007-June 2008.)* Ministry of Statistics and Programme Implementation, Government of India. May.

———. (2010c). "Migration in India", *NSSO Report 533, 64th Round (July 2007-June 2008)*. Ministry of Statistics and Programme Implementation, Government of India, June.

NCAER (2008). *Study on Perception of the Disadvantaged in Seven States in India*. National Council of Applied Economic Research (not yet published).

Okigbo, B. (1990). "Home Gardens in Tropical Africa", in K. Landauer and M. Brazil (eds.), *Tropical Home Gardens*. Tokyo, Japan: United Nations University Press.

Oxford Poverty and Human Development Initiative (OPHI) (2010). *Country Briefing: Multidimensional Poverty Index (MPI) At a Glance*. *OPHI Country Briefing*, July.

Prosterman, Roy (2010). *Comparative Perspective: House and Garden Plots to Alleviate Rural Poverty*. Rural Development Institute. *http://rural.nic.in/Presentation/IAY_PPT_05052010.pdf*

Prosterman R., R. Mitchell and T. Hanstad (eds.) (2009). *One Billion Rising Law, Land and the Alleviation of Global Poverty*. Lieden University Press.

Shah, Tushaar, Ashoki Gulati, P. Hemant, Ganga Shreedhar, R.C. Jain (2009). "Secret of Gujarat's Agrarian Miracle after 2000", *Economic & Political Weekly* XLIV(52), December 26.

Sharma, Alakh N. (2009). "Bihar Economic Status", *Bihar Times, September* 15. *http://praveendwivedi.wordpress.com/2009/05/15/bihar-economic-status-alakh-n-sharma-report/*

Singh, Abhishek, Sandip Chakraborty and Tarun K. Roy (2008). "Villages in India-How Relevant is it in the Context of Development?", *Asian Population Studies* 4(2).

Singh, D.P. (2009). "Poverty and Migration: Does Moving Help?", *India Urban Poverty Report 2009*. Oxford University Press.

Singh, Harsh (2010a). *Creating Vibrant Public-Private-Panchayat Partnership (PPPP) for Inclusive Growth through Inclusive Governance*. New Delhi: Academic Foundation.

———. (2010b). "Need for a New PPP-based Architecture for Skill Development of the Masses", OP-ED *The Hindu*, 28th May. *http://www.thehindu.com/opinion/op-ed/article432444.ece*

Soemarwoto, O. (1987). "Homegardens: A Traditional Agroforestry System with a Promising Future", in H. Steppler and P.K.R. Nair (eds.), *Agroforestry: A Decade of Development*. Nairobi: International Council for Research in Agroforestry.

tho Seeth, H., S. Chachnov and A. Surinov (1998). "Russian Poverty: Muddling Through Economic Transition with Garden Plots", *World Development* 26(9).

Tooley, James (2009). *The Beautiful Tree: A Personal Journey into How the World's Poorest People are Educating Themselves.* Washington DC: CATO Institute.

Vasey, D.E. (1985). "Household Gardens and their Niche in Port Moresby, Papua New Guinea", *Food and Nutrition Bulletin* 7(3).

World Bank (2005). *Bihar: Towards a Development Strategy.*